Then Again...
Annapolis, 1900–1965

Ecology conscious youngsters in Lindamoor
formed a neighborhood clean-up crew in the 1960s.
MdHR G 2140–344

[*front endleaf*]
Cornhill and Fleet streets were typical of the racially-
mixed neighborhoods that comprised much of Annapolis around the
turn of the century. By Henry Schaefer, c. 1895.
MdHR G 182–419

[*frontispiece*]
Wiegard's Confectionery on State Circle is remembered
fondly by long-time Annapolitans who still speak with enthusiasm of the cakes
and ice cream served there.
MdHR G 1890–621

[*back endleaf*]
Jonas Green Park was a favorite picnic spot for Annapolitans,
including this group in 1960 who enjoyed the vista of the old Severn River
bridge. By Marion Warren.
MdHR G 1890–10,151

Then Again. . .

Annapolis, 1900–1965

BY MAME WARREN

TIME EXPOSURES LIMITED
Annapolis, Maryland

1990

Other books by Mame Warren (with Marion E. Warren):

THE TRAIN'S DONE BEEN AND GONE: AN ANNAPOLIS PORTRAIT, 1859–1910

EVERYBODY WORKS BUT JOHN PAUL JONES: A PORTRAIT OF THE
U. S. NAVAL ACADEMY, 1845–1915

BALTIMORE: WHEN SHE WAS WHAT SHE USED TO BE, 1850–1935

MARYLAND TIME EXPOSURES, 1840–1940

CATALOGING DATA

Warren, Mame, 1950–
    Then again . . . Annapolis, 1900–1965.

        1. Annapolis—History—Pictorial Works. 2. Oral history.
    3. Photographs—History. 4. Photography, architectural.

LIBRARY OF CONGRESS CATALOG # 90-71343

ISBN 0-9627799-0-3 *casebound*

ISBN 0-9627799-1-1 *softcover*

This book was developed from an oral history project funded by the Maryland
Humanities Council, Inc., through a grant from the National Endowment for the
Humanities. The findings and conclusions contained in this volume do not
necessarily represent the views of the Maryland Humanities Council, Inc. or the
National Endowment for the Humanities.

*To Mary and Marion Warren, my mother and father, who
somehow knew that allowing a seven-year-old to stay up—just
once—until midnight would engender a special fondness for
history and for the town where I was born.*

The Warrens, Paul, Marion, Mame, Mary, and Nancy, the day after the
Colonial Ball. The memorable event took place November 23, 1958, in
the State House with everyone, including the few children who
attended, arrayed in colonial costumes.

Acknowledgments

Many, many people have contributed their time, energy, and treasures to this book. For once, though, it is easy to know whom to thank first. It was Sharie Valerio who suggested recording the stories of long-time Annapolitans—and I quickly realized that those stories would be the perfect complement to the photographs I had been collecting for a potential book. Sharie, in turn, brought Beth Whaley into the project, and soon the three of us were off with microphones in hand, interviewing what seemed like half of Annapolis' citizens. We called our overall project *The Annapolis I Remember*, and our primary focus was the collection of oral histories and historical photographs. That material became the source for much of the substance of this book. To Sharie and Beth, I offer my gratitude for their devotion.

Without the generous financial support of numerous benefactors, this effort would not have been possible. To the Maryland Humanities Council and the National Endowment for the Humanities, County Executive James Lighthizer and the Anne Arundel County Community Promotions Grants Program, the City of Annapolis and the Annapolis Fine Arts Foundation, the State Commission on the Capital City, Lionel Brooks, Historic Annapolis Foundation, St. John's College, Eastman Kodak Corporation, and William Johnson, grateful thanks for their support of *The Annapolis I Remember*.

Still others were early and unfailing champions of this effort, and their contributions have come in many forms. To Tom Roskelly, Flora Chambers, Jeff Bishop, Jack Carr, Pam Garland, George Phelps, Meg Clark, Brad Davidson, Keren Dement, Tom Florestano, Tom Marquardt, and Carl Snowden, my personal and heartfelt thanks.

The outstanding advisory board for *The Annapolis I Remember* project has offered excellent guidance. Peter Beckett, Philip Brown, Charles Camp, James Wesley Clark, Andrea Hammer, Phebe Jacobsen, Jane McWilliams, Barry Meiners, Ben Primer, Linda Shopes, Barbara Vandegrift, and Lori Wesley Alperin each contributed invaluable suggestions and challenged us to explore the deeper meanings and historical importance of the information we collected.

The Arundel Senior Assistance Programs, Inc. rendered a firm foundation for this project. In particular, Norbert Frankenberger, Red Waldron, Connie Panella, and Virginia Thomas were gracious with their time and energy. The Anne Arundel County Department of Aging was also a strong early proponent of *The Annapolis I Remember*, particularly Carol Baker and Trish McGarty.

From the Maryland State Archives, I received considerable professional support. Through the good graces of State Archivist Edward C. Papenfuse, I was permitted extended leave time from my position as curator of photographs. Other members of the staff who offered helpful ideas were Gregory Stiverson, Christopher Allan, and Lynne Browne. Numerous members of the staff of the Historic Annapolis Foundation shared a wealth of information with me, particularly Jean Russo and Linnell Bowen. I want to recognize them, and President Joseph Coale, for their kindness. The staff at the Banneker-Douglass Museum: Steven Newsome, Barbara Jackson, Bernadette Pulley-Pruitt, and Laurence Hurst, also welcomed me and gave considerable time and thought to this project.

Another group I want to acknowledge in a special way has no official title, but I have dubbed them The Lunch

After carefully draping herself with an array of portraits, Annapolitan Lena Thomas posed with a view camera, c. 1900.
MdHR G 2258–15

Bunch. These wonderful women invited me into their intimate circle several times and allowed me to explore their lively and highly entertaining memories of their Annapolis childhoods. Marge Dowsett, Pat Hayward, Ruby Miller, Dorothy Thomas, Marge Wells, and Eleanor O'Neill—I savored every moment with you.

The most important contributors, of course, were the Annapolitans (including a few who have escaped to other parts of the country) who participated in the interview process and those who loaned photographs for copying. Interviewees were Prudence Adams, Cleo Apostol, Marion Borsodi, Lionel Brooks, Robert H. Campbell, Jack Carr, Marita Carroll, Flora Chambers, Helen Chambers, James Wesley Clark, James B. Collins, Claudia Cullimore, Charles R. Dodds, Jimmy Dunleavy, Vera Engelke, Alexander J. Eucare, Lacey Evans, Lillian Fisher, Amelia Florestano, Nick Fotos, Margaret Green, Sonny Greengold, Charles Haste, Henry Holland, Carroll Hynson, Jr., Esther King, Helen Lacey, Buddy Levy, Jane McWilliams, William J. McWilliams, Ellen Moyer, Roger Moyer, George Phelps, Jane Phillips, Henry M. Robert III, Gina Rogers, Emily Rucker, Mary Lee Schab, Bernard E. Sears, Wendell Dean Sears, Walter B. Smith, Mary Wiseman, Margaret Worthington, and A. St. Clair Wright.

Interviewees who also contributed photographs were Tom Branzell, Virginia Chambers, Missy Weems Dodds, Marge Dowsett, Jack Flood, Bernard Gessner, Anna Greenberg, Bessie Gritz, Elmer M. Jackson, Jr., Peggy Kimbo, John Kramer, Emily Holland Peake, William Phelps, Sadie Levy Snyder, Lester Trott, Sharie Valerio, and Tom Worthington.

Barbara Baden Bentley, Morris Blum, Beatrice Britton, Philip Dodds, Harold Earle, Dorothy Egan, Kate Finkelstein, Veola Gantt, Eric Goldstein, John Hammond, Howard G. Hayman, Jr., Dermott Hickey, Thomas Chattle Hopkins, Jr., William P. Johnson, Miriam Jones, Herbert Kotzin, Gil McNew, Elizabeth McWethey, Max Ochs, Jerome Parks, Emma Pickett, Bernadette Pulley-Pruitt, John Russell, Annie Smith, Julia R. Thomas, Mary Tyler, Stu Whelan, Florine Williams, Leon Wolfe, and Robert Worden kindly shared their photographic treasures.

From the beginning, I have been blessed with a support staff who have made enormous contributions to this entire project. My trusted troop of volunteers: Chuck Dennis, Greg Halpin, Gladys Lambert, Helen Orme, Harrison Sayre, and Marguerite Smith, have ungrudgingly accomplished much of the drudge work to help keep this enormous operation under control. They have done so with good cheer and encouraged me when I felt overwhelmed. I also want to recognize the assistance and critical insight contributed by Amanda Merrill, who assured me that this undertaking is of interest to the younger generation as well as us old-timers.

Deborah Reid and her army of transcribers at Techni-Type deserve much of the credit for helping to keep this project on schedule. The many hours they spent translating the spoken word into written text allowed me to concentrate on other things with confidence that the fruit of their work would be both precise and accurate.

Most of all, I want to thank my father, Marion Warren, who not only gave unlimited access to the thousands of photographs he took in Annapolis from 1947 through 1965, but also spent countless hours in the studio copying hundreds of images, and then countless more in the darkroom making hundreds of prints for this book. His unique contribution is of inestimable value and is most gratefully appreciated.

I am also very much obliged to David Williams at Electronic Publishing Solutions for his meticulous work setting the type and his understanding and tolerance as changes were made. Credit for the quality of the printed pages in this volume goes to George Shenk and the craftsmen at Whitmore Printing. I am indebted to them for their painstaking care and attention to every detail.

The flow of the following pages reflects the artistry of master designer Gerard A. Valerio. Working with Gerry is always an adventure in the pursuit of perfection. From his initial suggestion to organize the book chronologically to his inspired arrangements of photographs that counterbalance one another in impact and theme, Gerry has once again demonstrated his genius.

Eric Goldstein has been my right hand man during much of this endeavor. His extensive knowledge of Annapolis history has been invaluable, and his constant probing and questioning have enriched the scholarly content of this volume. Among other tasks, he located many of the entries in the chronology, found present-day street addresses, and assembled the index and bibliography.

Jane McWilliams' official capacity in this enterprise has been to serve as editor and to remind me of all the rules of grammar and punctuation my sixth grade teacher tried so hard to instill in me. I am grateful for every comma and semicolon, and if any errors persist, no doubt they

On February 20, 1909, McDowell Hall, on St. John's College campus, was virtually destroyed by fire. Restoration of the building took more than a year. MdHR G 182–1608

are the result of my own stubborn resistance to her corrections. Jane has been much more than just an editor, however, because her knowledge and experience of Annapolis are so abundant and her sensitivity to the subtleties of the spoken word is so perceptive. Her contributions are beyond measure. More than all of this, I am thankful for her constant enthusiasm and friendship.

Finally, and most especially, I want to express my unreserved gratitude to my husband, Henry Harris, for his patience, understanding, and encouragement every step of this long and winding way. Henry is always my first and favorite photo critic and has helped to manage much of this production. This obsessed author could not wish for a better friend.

Reflections

Blending pictures and stories about life in Annapolis from 1900 to 1965—it seemed like a simple enough concept a little over a year ago when this project began. The idea of fashioning a sequel to *The Train's Done Been and Gone: An Annapolis Portrait 1859–1910* (a book co-authored by my father, Marion Warren, and me in 1976) had long been gestating in my mind. When it dawned on me to merge my historical photographs with actual living voices, I suddenly felt compelled to make this book right now. Simple logic told me that the people who could relate stories about Annapolis long ago would not be around forever. As one narrator, Dean Sears, cautions,

> *We never talked too much about that. My mother was from Shroudsburg, Pennsylvania. How did my father ever meet my mother? Because in those days they only had horses and buggies. They were married back in, I don't know, maybe 1909, 1910, something like that. We never did know. You know, you always wanted to know, but never asked. My father died, and we never did ask it. And there's nobody left to tell us, because all their families are gone now.*

I started by looking for prototypes of the book I envisioned—examples of other local history books that gave equal emphasis to photographic illustrations and text derived from oral history interviews. I found oral history books, and picture books, but none that integrated the two in the balanced way that I had in mind.

In my naiveté, I had no appreciation for the complexity of the task I had set for myself. Now that it's done, however, I have no regrets. I am more convinced than ever that this presentation makes sense. I know from experience that photographs make history accessible to a wide audience, so it was important to me to give considerable emphasis to illustrations. At the same time, I hope readers will give equal consideration to the wisdom that

St. Anne's Church and Church Circle in snowstorm, 1954.
MdHR G 1890–248A

emerges from the oral history interviews. At times, the connection between the spoken word and the visual image is uncanny, and it is my intent to make those relationships readily understood.

For almost twenty years, I have devoted much of my life to collecting vintage photographs, not as art, but as documents of our culture. The practice of oral history, on the other hand, is relatively new to me. At the beginning of this project, I had excellent training, but little experience in the field. It didn't take long to become an enthusiastic proponent of the technique: the information gathered is so fresh, so uncensored, and so human in its concerns.

The observations quoted in this book are derived from more than seventy interviews conducted over ten months in 1989 and 1990 by Beth Whaley, Sharie Valerio, and myself. Together with more than eight hundred photographs I located and had copied, these interviews form the nucleus of *The Annapolis I Remember* project. The oral history tapes, transcripts, and the photographs are now a permanent collection at the Maryland State Archives. In addition to this book, a theatrical presentation and a traveling exhibition that also blend stories and images of Annapolis during the early part of this century have been produced as part of this project.

It is my hope that this book reflects back as closely as possible what was contributed in words and pictures by the people of Annapolis. In my selection of quotations, I have tried, as much as possible, to keep my own point of view to myself and instead to let all the many voices that make up this community have an opportunity to express their sentiments. The emphasis placed on certain themes mirrors what I believe I heard in the interviews. I do not agree with everything that is said in the commentaries that follow. I assume that most readers will take exception to at least one idea or thought that I have chosen to quote. My goal is to give expression to many views, to provoke thought, to remind us that we live in a diverse community.

Very little editing has been done to the words of the narrators. We have added punctuation and corrected grammar only when absolutely necessary for comprehension or clarity. Readers should be aware that the spoken word has little in common with carefully composed written text. Local slang is used liberally, and the result sounds clearly like voices speaking. In fact, reading the quotations aloud often adds to this sense of immediacy and the clear impression that a real person is the source of thoughts expressed.

In an effort to have the narration that follows speak for itself, and to allow the reader to concentrate on the relationship between the photographs and the stories, I have decided to make the quotations anonymous. Those who are curious about exactly who said what can easily follow the reference numeral to the endnotes in the back of the book. It is my intent, however, that the voices on the pages will form a chorus that speaks for all of Annapolis, with fondness, and humor, and insight.

Occasionally the breadth of some of the memories we explored was startling. Tom Worthington, for example, could reach back two generations with ease. As if it were yesterday, he rekindled the drama of a fire that took place October 21, 1883:

> My grandfather Thomas remembered the big fire down on Market Space, where a man was killed. It was a big commercial building that dated back to the revolutionary war days. My grandfather was a member of the fire company, and they still were using the hand pumper. And this was a terrible fire and the Naval Academy had gotten a steam pumper, and fortunately they brought that out and helped them put out the fire. But my grandfather said that he was going to do everything he could to see that Annapolis got a steam pumper, too, because he thought he'd killed himself pumping that hand pumper.

Still others offered poignant stories handed down by oral tradition of how their parents or grandparents first came to Annapolis and how they achieved success in the community. Sonny Greengold remembers his parents' early advertising techniques:

> Then when my mama came here from Russia, my parents opened up the store at 50 West Street. That's right on the corner of Gott's Court Alley and West Street. My mother and father rented that little tailor shop. And they would sit in that window sometimes until two o'clock in the morning to make out they were busy, pressing their own clothes.

During the period that this book covers, the black segment of Annapolis comprised a fairly steady thirty-three percent of the population. Thus, about one-third of the narrators interviewed were black: their commentaries are interspersed throughout the book. There is also a small but significant Filipino presence in Annapolis, and I was fortunate to find a particularly eloquent spokesman for that group. I have attempted to be somewhat color blind as I matched stories with pictures; sometimes a black narrator comments on a photograph where whites pose for the camera, and vice versa. That level of parity was not possible in the selection of photographs, however. Photographs of blacks during the early part of this century seem to be rare, and there appear to be virtually none of Filipino families. I was able to locate only a few previously unpublished images of blacks made before the 1940s, when Thomas Baden, Jr., took up photography—and in so doing, created an intimate visual record of life in Annapolis' black community, from Carr's Beach to his own dinner table.

Sometimes there were stories that were retold in various versions by numerous narrators but were not easily illustrated. Take the phenomenon of the "blind eel," for example. Those who put so much value on waterfront property today might be surprised to learn that at one time Spa Creek was a less than desirable address. Bobby Campbell explains,

> The City Dock was a great cesspool. The sewer lines went down to the end of every street, and they dumped in Spa Creek, in Severn River, in Back Creek, all the sewer lines, all the sewage. When we would swim, we'd just take our arm and move the stuff out of the way. We called them blind eels. We'd move the blind eels out of the way. Talk about the ecology. The alewives would come up and feed on the sewage. The bluefish would come up and feed on the alewives. We'd go down and catch the bluefish and bring them home and fry them and eat them. So that's the ecology. And I'm still here.

Not surprisingly, the city's peninsular setting gave expression to many other stories relating to the water. Time and again, bittersweet memories stirred poignant laments about the current plight of the Chesapeake Bay.

Slippery Hill includes Revell, Conduit, and Market streets. Some Annapolitans claim that the name reflects the steepness of the hills in the neighborhood, viewed *above* from Spa Creek, with a house under construction on Market Street, November 1884.
MdHR G 2140–97A

Perhaps members of faculty families, this group of fashionable girls posed for a photographer visiting the Naval Academy, c. 1867. MdHR G 2140–357

Today, Annapolitans are accustomed to a more complete profile of St. Mary's Church than the view *above*. The photograph was taken sometime after 1858 when the church was built, but before its steeple was constructed. MdHR G 2140–414

An equally unusual image was made of St. Anne's Church with its steeple incomplete, *above*, seen from Main Street c. 1859–1865. This rare *carte de visite* view is among the earliest photographs known to have been made in Annapolis. MdHR G 2140–425

Charles Haste recalls,

> *That's when you should have seen the Chesapeake Bay or the Severn River. I mean, you could just ride out there and see the fish. You're not even catching them. I mean, you could carry on a conversation with them. They were so big, and so close, and so clean. That's when oysters and everything was really great. In the forties, in the thirties, it was like a rich harvest field of fish and oysters and clams and what have you. It was nice. It was healthier, and it was better. I'm sorry we can't get it back.*

This ability to pluck food from the creeks surrounding virtually every neighborhood kept many lower income families nourished during lean years, especially during the Depression. And it was often the children, now seventy years old and the subjects of our interviews, who were the food gatherers. Again, Bobby Campbell remembers,

> *When I was a boy, two men could go out on a tong boat and catch thirty, forty bushels a day, and if they were real good and struck it good, they could catch as many as sixty bushel a day. These oystermen don't get sixty bushel in a week in the dredge boats, hardly, today. I could go right here in the City Dock or down at the foot of Prince George Street, even after World War II, and in a couple of hours, catch a bushel of crabs. I could stand down there a week now and couldn't catch a bushel of crabs.*

By the late 1930s, some enterprising local businessmen had begun to explore the possibility of developing Annapolis as a yachting center. Over the ensuing years, a subtle, but ultimately dramatic, evolution took place in Annapolitans' perspective of the Bay. By the 1950s and 1960s, more residents began to view the water not as a source of sustenance, but as a source of pleasure. Now, when Annapolitans consider why they choose to live here, their thoughts are often more philosophical. Sharie Valerio muses,

> *One thing that happens when you're raised in Annapolis is that the water becomes a part of your visual and spiritual being. You take it for granted that you will see water every day of your life probably, if you're an Annapolitan and you go out.*
>
> *And I didn't know that that was part of me. I didn't get it until I went to Ohio with my husband to visit*

in-laws, and I got claustrophobic, and I really didn't know what was the matter with me. We were there for a week, and about two or three days into the week, I said, "Where's the water? Isn't there any water around here? Is there a lake or something?" And I realized that I'm not used to that. And going across the Eastport bridge or the Weems Creek bridge, Severn River bridge, every day of my life, all my life, I'm used to that, and I think that gives you a wonderful sense, you know. It's a beautiful thing to have as a part of your inner self.

Annapolitans enjoyed distinct economic benefits from their immediate environs. Unlike many less fortunate communities, Annapolis did not suffer dramatically during the Depression years. With a constant food source in the Chesapeake Bay and steady employment at the Naval Academy, Annapolis, our narrators assured us repeatedly, was a very good place to live in the thirties. Even if the wage earner in the family was a streetsweeper,

Soon after it was established in 1845, the U. S. Naval Academy began acquiring land adjacent to its original site where Spa Creek meets the Severn River. As a result, the city of Annapolis lost considerable acreage over the years. This panorama looking toward College Creek was taken from New Quarters in 1875, just after the academy purchased the area known as Lockwoodville. Within months the houses seen on Wagner Street were demolished. MdHR G 1890–3950

The Naval Academy was the single largest source of employment for the local populace for more than a century. Even during the Depression Annapolis' economy was relatively secure because government jobs were rarely threatened. *Above,* laborers pose with their tools in 1875 on newly acquired academy land. MdHR G 2140–415

In 1880, J. Federleicht's shoe store was located on Market Space in the Wallace-Davidson-Johnson building, an eighteenth century structure. The building was destroyed in a dramatic fire on October 21, 1883. MdHR G 1890–3153

there were plenty of crabcakes and oysters, and a few extra dollars could be made on weekends by renting rooms to "hop girls" who came to town for events at the Naval Academy.

The word *cosmopolitan* kept coming up in descriptions of the town's ambience. Having two institutions of higher education in the city provided extraordinary amenities for a town the size of Annapolis. Peggy Kimbo remembers fondly, "St. John's was our playground and so was the academy. I thought we were rich kids because of where we could play."

New blood, new ideas, and new perspectives arrived with the ever-changing population of the Naval Academy, both midshipmen and faculty families. Every age group was affected. The grand dames of Annapolis society were delighted to have well-traveled guests at their garden parties, and the children in both public and private schools had students in their geography classes who actually had been to California, England, and Japan. As Lester Trott explains:

> *The interesting part growing up in the area was that it was very sophisticated education-wise because you always had the influence of the Naval Academy through their children, navy juniors. And the navy juniors would come into the system, the educational system especially, and bring in new ideas, what had happened, where things were, what things were like in other parts of the world. And it was sort of a pseudo-education in the fact that the local people, who never traveled or anything like that, were given a broader view of what was beyond the limits of Annapolis.*

There were also local personalities who obviously added greatly to the local temperament. The names of Oscar Warmkessel, Sam Lorea, and "Snake" Baker resounded throughout the interviews. Oscar, in particular, caught my fancy, but unfortunately no portraits of him seem to survive. His story, though, has become legend. Tom Worthington summons an enchanting image:

> *Oscar Warmkessel slept down in the powerhouse at the Naval Academy in the wintertime, where it was warm, and summertime, he'd make a little shack up on the banks of Graveyard Creek—College Creek—and he would live there. He made it out of cardboard and wood and so on. He would go around to the various stores and restaurants on Main Street and he would sweep.*

> *You gave him a broom and he would sweep as long as you wanted him to sweep. And they would give him a little bit of money and sort of watch out for him. He would wear a blue watchcap, and an old pea coat.*

> *And if it hadn't been for one marvelous talent, nobody would have remembered him much. He was just sort of the village idiot until the creek froze over. Then he became a star because he was a fabulous ice-skater. He could do all of these things that you see people in the Ice Capades do. He could do figure-eights and twirls and leaps and all this sort of thing, and we kids were just goggle-eyed as we watched Oscar go through this tremendous repertoire. And I never figured out how he learned to do that, because it seemed like otherwise he would be lucky if he could walk, much less skate. Oscar was around all through the thirties when I was a child and into the early forties. I think he died about then.*

Other long-time residents assured me that Oscar always slept by the front door of T. Kent Green's pharmacy on Main Street; still others said that he—in a friendly sort of way—broke into people's furnace rooms and slept there in the winter. As a thank-you, he would stoke the fire before he left in the morning.

For most, this Annapolis has become only a fond memory. "We aren't a neighborhood anymore; people just live in houses," laments Marion Borsodi. But if, after perusing the following pages, a few readers are inspired to pull the old rocking chairs out onto the front porch and invite the neighbors over for a chat, I will consider my mission accomplished.

Chronology

1803
Asbury United Methodist Church is established.

1830
Census registers 2,623 persons in Annapolis.

1840
December 25: First train of the Annapolis & Elkridge Railroad travels between Annapolis and the Washington branch of the Baltimore & Ohio Railroad.

1845
U. S. Naval Academy is established.

1847
U. S. Naval Academy expands with purchase of additional land along Severn River.

1853
U. S. Naval Academy enlarged for the second time with acquisition of land later occupied by the Victorian chapel and Blake Row. Also, a high hill on the Severn River acquired and leveled.

1858
St. Mary's Roman Catholic Church construction begins.
February 14: St. Anne's Protestant Episcopal Church destroyed by fire that started in the furnace. Reconstruction begins in 1859; steeple completed in 1865. Building costs $21,500 without steeple; steeple costs more than $8,000. First services held in summer of 1859.

1859
January 7: Annapolis Gas-Light Company incorporated. By 1888, there are five miles of underground pipe.

1861
U. S. Naval Academy students move to Newport, Rhode Island, for the duration of the Civil War. Naval Academy and St. John's College transformed into army hospitals.

1866
U. S. Naval Academy expands for the third time when Maryland's original Governor's Mansion purchased to become the library. Porter Row built between the mansion and the water. Total land added, four acres. Present Governor's Mansion begun on State Circle under the administration of Governor Thomas Swann.

1867
U. S. Naval Academy expands for the fourth time when ten acres along College Creek are bought from St. John's College.

1868
U. S. Naval Academy buys Strawberry Hill, sixty-seven acres adjacent to grounds of the naval hospital. Part of this land used as burial ground by 1876 and connected with lot bought from St. John's by a wooden bridge over College Creek.
First Eastport bridge built across Spa Creek.

1872
Experimental battery established across the Severn River on site of Fort Madison. By 1888, known as the Naval Ordnance Proving Grounds. Battery contains eighty-five acres where experiments in explosives, rifles, and ordnance are systematically conducted.

1874
U. S. Naval Academy enlarged for the sixth time with purchase of four acres, called Lockwoodville, on the water between College Avenue, Hanover and Wagner streets. All but one of the Lockwoodville tenements removed by 1876.

1875
June 7: Cornerstone of St. Martin's Lutheran Church on Francis Street laid.

1876
Mount Moriah A.M.E. Church established.

1877
Construction begins on St. Anne's chapel at Prince George and East streets from a design furnished by Professor Oliver of the U. S. Naval Academy. First story completed in 1878 and used for services. Chapel unfinished until 1885 when family of Alexander Randall pays for its completion as a memorial to him. Total building costs about nine thousand dollars.

1880
Mayor's Report, issued on July 1, declares that "A continuation of the plan of permitting cesspools to honeycomb our city must be discontinued,…from the porous nature of our soil and the indiscriminate use of privy sinks, the water in our pumps has become poisoned and unfit for use."

1883
October 21: Major fire burns the entire block between Main Street and Cornhill Street on Market Space. Losses include two lives, the Wallace-Davidson-Johnson building, ten homes, and numerous businesses. Photographer Charles R. Martin's studio destroyed. Total loss, ninety thousand dollars.

1888
Annapolis has four public schools (with separations for sex and race), three parochial schools, and five private schools. Average attendance at public schools is 450 white and 300 black. In the public schools, there are 20 teachers for white children, 6 for black children. St. Mary's school taught by 12 sisters with 130 white students and 190 black students in separate school buildings.
Eastport Post Office established. Community name suggested by Charles J. Murphy, a native of Eastport, Maine.

1899
March 28: Construction of the new U. S. Naval Academy buildings begins from plans drawn by architect Ernest Flagg. Virtually all old buildings, including Fort Severn, eventually torn down.

1900
February 11: *Mayor's Report* announces that the sewer system has been completed, the dock deepened, and West Street paved from Church Circle beyond Colonial Avenue.
March 24: *Evening Capital* reports that work is underway at the Naval Academy to

enclose a lagoon as an anchorage for ships attached to the academy.

April 4: Bay Ridge transformed into religious Chautauqua. Opens to public May 31. The newspaper relates that "No colored persons are employed on any part of the grounds, and the company prohibits colored excursionists from entering the place."

August 23: Severn Glass Works in Eastport enlarged and remodeled. Old ovens taken down and replaced by seven larger and more convenient ovens with double the capacity.

November 10: Pinkney-Callahan House, fully furnished, moved three hundred feet across College Avenue to make room for Court of Appeals building. Six workers and a superintendent accomplish work with six skids and seventy-five jack-screws. Job not completed until January 23 due to bad weather. College Avenue blocked for fifteen days.

1901

December 22: Oyster boats put into port three days before Christmas and remain until March 20. Bay frozen from Tilghman Island to Baltimore.

1902

January 1: New Annapolis Post Office and Customs House opens at 1 Church Circle eleven months after ground was broken.

March 20: Court of Appeals building cornerstone laid.

May 18: Colonial Theatre opens on Conduit Street.

July 23: Fire destroys St. Martin's Church, Wiegard's Confectionery, and other buildings on Francis Street and State Circle.

1903

Carvel Hall Hotel opens.

1904

April 17: One of the most destructive fires in Annapolis to date originates at R. G. Chaney's livery stable on West Street; fourteen residences consumed. Loss of thirty thousand dollars. Midshipmen and marines help fight fire.

December 9: Work on dome of U. S. Naval Academy chapel, begun four months prior, almost completed.

1906

Land Office on State House grounds torn down.

December 21: Mob breaks into county jail and lynches Henry Davis, a black man, by hanging him from a large chestnut tree over College Creek seven days after he had raped a white woman. Davis confessed to the crime. The next day, the *Evening Capital* reports that "all reasonable precautions were taken.…No one expressed any open sorrow or indignation at the affair and many respectable colored persons said that Davis had received what he deserved."

1907

April 8: New bridge to Eastport opens. Features sidewalks for foot passengers. Newspaper declares that "Everybody in Eastport is wearing the smile that won't come off and everybody in Annapolis is equally pleased."

1908

March 25: Official opening of the WB&A electric line intracity route.

May 28: First services held in new Naval Academy chapel. Building cost $374,194. *Mayor's Report* for 1909 reveals that between April 1 and December 31, 1908, 313,000 adults and 1,876 children rode on the Washington, Baltimore & Annapolis Railroad. Half-hourly service between Annapolis and Baltimore available.

Sewers laid on Franklin, Dean, Bladen, and Newman streets, Southgate and Cheston avenues, and O'Bryan's Alley. Dean Street graded, curbed, and shelled. Rubble-stone laid and concrete curb installed on Duke of Gloucester from Newman Street to the Eastport bridge. Bladen and Martin streets paved with vitrified brick. Franklin Street extended, concrete curb and gutter laid, and macadam surface put on street.

1909

Area of the city is 349.93 acres, as determined by City Engineer J. C. Little.

February 20: McDowell Hall at St. John's College burns. Probable cause, defective wiring. Midshipmen come to help fight the fire, marines to control the crowd. Insured for only $20,900. Restoration takes more than a year.

June 17: Fort Severn at the U. S. Naval Academy demolished despite vigorous protests from preservationists.

1910

August 10: Steamer *Idler* begins service across Bay from City Dock, with connection to WB&A trains at foot of Main Street. Twelve passengers make first trip. One round-trip a day planned.

December 1: Although not yet complete, new Emergency Hospital opens for inspection by public. Features three stories with basement kitchen, wards for men and women, children's ward and private rooms, two operating rooms, bath rooms separate from toilet rooms. Heated with hot water, lighted with electricity.

1911

April 14: Cedar Park advertised in *Evening Capital*. Covers thirty-three acres with a "commanding view of Annapolis overlooking College Creek on one side and rolling, undulating land on the other." Suggested as an ideal place for a summer home. Located on the WB&A line with its own station.

June: Second fire at Chaney's livery stable at Colonial Avenue and West Street. Thousands watch from lawn of James Munroe's house across the street. Fifty-two horses die, four survive. Livery wagons, hacks, and carts burn. Telephone service disrupted for part of the city.

August 9: Colonial Theatre re-opens after three months of improvements. All seats ten cents. Painted deep maroon with gold trimmings. Three vaudeville acts with movie every night, personally censored by new manager to assure that they are clean. Amenities include toilets, telephones, and a maid in the ladies' room.

September 7: First flight from Naval Academy to Washington, D. C., made by Lieutenant John Rodgers in one hour and twenty minutes. Newspaper reports "it is the first flight ever made by a naval officer to amount to anything." Rodgers lands on the Mall in Washington and all traffic stops.

November: Three airplanes delivered to Annapolis and kept at experimental station for naval aviation training. Frequent articles in the *Evening Capital* refer to pilots as "Bird Men." Operations move to Pensacola, Florida, in 1912.

1912

May 17: First woman doctor arrives in Annapolis. Dr. Frances E. Weitzman, graduate in medicine and surgery from a Philadelphia medical school, opens an office at 111 Conduit Street.

October 1: Captured Spanish cruiser, *Reina Mercedes*, arrives to serve as station ship at the Naval Academy.

1913
May 16: *Evening Capital* reports that several merchants have "paving fever." Abraham Greengold and Abraham Miller on West Street, Leon Gottlieb on Main Street, and the Fashion Tailoring Shop on Maryland Avenue have installed cement sidewalks.
June 24: Southbound Short Line freight train falls through opened bridge into Severn River. Crew escapes unhurt. Engine later retrieved; service disrupted for nearly a week.

1914
May: St. John's student shot and killed in hazing incident.

1915
August 4: Worst storm in city's history hits Annapolis at night, causing flooding, blowing off roofs, destroying buildings. Damage totals $250,000. Bodies found floating above ground in St. Anne's Cemetery. Destroys bridge between Highland Beach and Arundel on the Bay.

1918
March 16: *Evening Capital* reports that Secretary of the Navy Josephus Daniels has declared Annapolis a dry zone. Saloons to close by 4 P.M. Saturday (before working men have a chance to have a final "blow out"). No liquor to be sold within a five-mile radius of any naval installation. Ruling applies only to saloons. Breaking the law punishable by fine of not more than one thousand dollars or twelve months in jail. One saloon keeper mounts a sign reading, "Don't ask me what I am going to do; what the hell are *you* going to do?"
October: Hundreds infected with the Spanish influenza. *Evening Capital* recounts that "At Green's drug store the line extended into the street one night this week and some had to wait an hour and a half for their turn to have their prescription put up. Such a thing was never known in Annapolis before." Schools close on October 3 because 288 cases of flu reported in the grammar school. Many people die.
November 20: St. Anne's chapel at corner of Prince George and East streets purchased for

nine thousand dollars by Kneseth Israel congregation for use as a synagogue.

1919
January 17: Colonial Theatre destroyed by fire shortly after 1 A.M. Several businesses damaged. Watching the fire from a nearby rooftop, a Naval Academy candidate falls three stories and lands on his feet.
February 28: John Snowden hanged at Anne Arundel County Courthouse for allegedly murdering Lottie Mae Brandon. Last hanging in Annapolis. Weeks of controversy surround Snowden's hanging, with many believing in his innocence. After the hanging, an anonymous correspondent claims responsibility for the murder in a letter to the *Evening Capital*.
June 19: The ferryboat *Governor Emerson C. Harrington*, first to carry automobiles to Claiborne on the Eastern Shore, leaves from King George Street terminus.

1920
St. John's College team wins national lacrosse championship for second time.

1921
January: Public library opens in Assembly Rooms on Duke of Gloucester Street.
February: Maryland Public Service Commission approves merger of the Short Line Railroad and the WB&A.

1923
St. John's College abolishes compulsory military training. Administration changes; most of the old faculty resigns. New system of free electives established.
Elizabeth Carter, first policewoman hired by city, paid $50. Male officers paid $1,020 annually. In 1924, Ms. Carter paid $300.

1924
Summer: Severn River bridge, second on site, completed.

1927
There are 150 trains in and out of Annapolis daily, one ferry line from Annapolis to the Eastern Shore connecting by train to Ocean City, and one steamboat line from Baltimore to Annapolis and the river landings, according to the official program of the Maryland State Firemen's Association Convention held in Annapolis.

1928
May 15: Thousands attend Colonial Day festivities, including President Calvin Coolidge. Celebration begins with a lacrosse game at St. John's College, followed by numerous tableaux and reenactments of historical scenes. Historic homes opened to the public, and a Colonial Ball takes place in the State House.

1930
Census statistics show a population of 12,531. Retail business in excess of $7,877,785 at 220 retail stores, which give full-time employment to 627 men and women. Chain stores account for fifteen percent of retail businesses, and independents eighty-two percent. There are 74 food-oriented stores, including 40 grocery stores, 9 meat markets, and many bakeries; and 28 automotive-related businesses: 10 sell vehicles, 6 sell accessories, tires, and batteries, 7 are filling stations, and 5 are garages. Fifteen eating places, excluding hotels, boardinghouses, and drug stores, employ 59 people full-time. Fourteen are listed as lunch rooms and only one as a restaurant.
Amoco station built on Main Street at City Dock.
Fish market torn down at head of City Dock.
January 28: Classrooms at elementary school on Green Street gutted by fire.
February 11: High school on Green Street catches fire, causing $25,000 in damages. Fire starts on third floor during school hours. The *Evening Capital* reports that "Since the grammar school fire the heating plant in the high school has been kept very hot…to keep both buildings warm."
July: Ferry service to Matapeake on the Eastern Shore begins. New, shorter route employs three diesel-powered boats: the *John M. Dennis*, the *Governor Albert C. Ritchie*, and the *Governor Harry W. Nice*.

1933
August 23: Hurricane causes great damage. Knights of Columbus hut on Spa Creek off Compromise Street destroyed, pier at Severn Boat Club washed away, *Reina Mercedes* wharf at Naval Academy ruined, Prince George Street flooded up to Randall Street. People are evacuated in rowboats.
September 13: Annapolis votes six to one for repeal of Prohibition.

1935

August 20: Passenger service on the WB&A Railroad comes to an end. In July 1935, the Baltimore & Annapolis Railroad incorporated and acquired some WB&A equipment. The new company strengthens the bridge across the Severn River and changes the Baltimore terminus to Camden Station and the Annapolis one to the Bladen Street station.

1936

January 8: Governor's Mansion being transformed from its original Victorian architecture into neo-Georgian style. Governor Harry W. Nice asks "the people of the State to suspend their judgment upon what I have done until the Government House, now exteriorly presenting an object of beauty, in the wisdom of the Legislature, may have been completed."

January 8: Company for the Restoration of Colonial Annapolis incorporated, and three hundred citizens attend dinner at Carvel Hall. Annual dues one dollar. George Forbes suggests that Andrew Carnegie should buy the entire city and restore it to its colonial appearance. "If each rich man would take a house to restore, it would solve the problem."

1937

Arundel Bus Company sets first route from Tyler Avenue over the old Eastport bridge, "through town, over the railroad tracks to an almost undeveloped Cedar Park and West Annapolis."

September 22: Great books program, called the New Program, begins at St. John's College. Of forty-five freshmen who enter in 1937, twenty enroll in the New Program. Old program continues for students in sophomore, junior, and senior classes.

November 21: Carvel Hall fire destroys two top floors of new wings, causing fifty thousand dollars damage. Little damage to Paca House. Midshipmen help fight fire. Extinguished in one and one-half hours. Hotel closes temporarily.

1938

Survey conducted by Annapolis Housing Authority reveals a city population of 9,354, excluding the Naval Academy. There are 1,759 white, 938 black, and 15 Filipino or Chinese families. Sub-standard housing comprises 38.4 percent of available shelter, occupied by 1,042 families. Of these families, 812 are black, 217 white, 13 Filipino or Chinese. Structures with no electric lights comprise 13 percent of all housing, 27 percent have no indoor flush toilets, 28.9 percent no bath or shower. Typical "slum" house rents for $15.00–$17.50 per month, with an additional eight or nine dollars for utilities.

January: Group of Annapolis businessmen, all members of the Annapolis Yacht Club, incorporate the Yacht Basin Company and open the docks with 124 moorings to the public. Plans are to make Annapolis the yachting capital of the inland waterways system.

May: Property purchased for first state office building in Annapolis includes ten dwellings, a hotel, and a church on College Avenue and Bladen Street. Board of Public Works appropriates one million dollars for the project.

1940

Naval Academy begins to prepare for war by cutting Christmas vacation to one day. Extra plebes entering in September swell total of midshipmen to 2,600. Reserve candidates enter in February and are commissioned as reserve ensigns in May.

Four Rivers Garden Club begins program to plant 688 trees in town. Fifty trees planned for Duke of Gloucester, Charles, Cathedral, Market, Revell and Shipwright streets.

Life magazine publishes an article about St. John's College with photographs by Alfred Eisenstaedt. Enrollment of ninety-three freshmen in 1940 contrasts with forty in 1938 and fifty-four in 1939. For the first time since the New Program began, there are more applicants than the college can handle. Class of 1944 referred to as the *Life* class.

Summer: College Creek Terrace, designed by local architect Earle Harder, opens as public housing. Units rent for $17.25–$18.50 per month, including utilities.

1941

First classmen at Naval Academy graduate on February 7. Underclassmen attend only the Farewell Ball, otherwise they study as usual. Summer cruises dropped for second classmen.

Spring: Several blocks between King George and Prince George streets, commonly known as Hell Point, annexed by U. S. Naval Academy. Annapolis Housing Authority had had options on thirty properties and had planned to build defense housing project for navy workers and enlisted men. Also, twenty-two acres added to Hospital Point by pumping silt from the Severn River into a steel-bulkheaded area along shore. Holland Field and seven and a half acres behind Thompson Stadium also added. U. S. Naval Academy now totals 245 acres.

June: Last seniors educated under old program and first seniors of New Program graduate together in 149th commencement exercises at St. John's College. One old program senior plans to return to enter New Program as freshman.

December 7: U. S. Naval Academy becomes off-limits to all but those who live or work in the yard for the duration of World War II.

1942

Spring: United Service Organizations (USO), for enlisted men on duty at the *Reina Mercedes*, opens in abandoned church at corner of Maryland Avenue and Prince George Street. Operated by YMCA; features dances, movies, roller skating.

Recreation center on Compromise Street built on site of tenements on Newman Street. City contributes $42,000 and the federal government $77,000, with an agreement that building will be used as USO facility for ten years.

1943

Ferry service discontinued from King George Street. New terminal at Sandy Point shortens trip to the Eastern Shore by twenty-five minutes.

Black students at segregated Bates High School study agriculture. School operates chicken houses, cultivates fifteen acres. Produce from gardens canned by girls for use in cafeteria.

1945

June 12: Naval Academy threatens to takeover St. John's College. Mayor William McCready announces in the Baltimore *Evening Sun*: "Today, with the academy apparently about to take over the St. John's College property,…we want to be able to say to the navy, 'Come on in and take more—take all you want to.'"

1947

January 28: Five hundred and eighteen parking meters installed at a cost of $50.50 each.

Mayor McCready declares that they "will pay for themselves in one year."

June: Eastport bridge, opened in 1907, replaced by new bridge to Sixth Street. William T. Branzell, tender of old bridge for twenty-six years, succeeded by Edward R. Norfolk. New bridge costs $667,000, is 832 feet long, has low water clearance beneath the lift span of seventeen feet. Roadway twenty-six feet wide curb to curb, with six-foot sidewalks on either side. Work began March 14, 1946, by McLean Contracting Company of Baltimore. Chinquapin Round Road built to help ease traffic on the bridge. First Annapolis–Newport Yacht Race.

1949

May: Tercentenary celebration commemorates the founding of the city.

1950

Anne Arundel County Courthouse annex built at a cost of $910,000.

February 5: Final passenger train to Annapolis arrives at Bladen Street station at 1:55 A.M. Freight service continues for eighteen years hauling coal for the Naval Academy, lumber and building supplies for local dealers, paper, beer, and general merchandise for other customers. Bridge across Severn deemed unsafe in 1968 and all rail service to Annapolis ceases.

1951

January 1: Annexation of West Annapolis, Wardour, Cedar Park, Germantown, Homewood, Eastport, Tyler Avenue, Forest Hills, Fairfax, Truxtun Heights, and Parole makes Annapolis the fourth largest city in Maryland. Nine thousand citizens added, making a total of twenty-five thousand in city. Area expands from .737 to 5.55 square miles. City council enlarged to sixteen aldermen, with two aldermen from each ward.

March 30: Carvel Hall Hotel's second fire, caused by smoldering cigarette in laundry chute, ruins kitchen wing. Two firemen, Dutch Britton and W. H. Stevens, injured. Paca House escapes damage.

Women admitted to St. John's College for the first time following a proposal by President Richard Weigle.

1952

Chesapeake Bay bridge opened and ferry service discontinued.

Historic Annapolis, Inc. founded.

Governor Theodore R. McKeldin and Mayor Arthur Ellington at the ribbon cutting ceremony for the opening of Rowe Boulevard in 1954. MdHR G 1890–30,222C

1954

November: Elizabeth, Queen Mother of Great Britain, visits Annapolis.

Rowe Boulevard opened.

1957

B&A Railroad station on Bladen Street torn down.

January 15: Governor Theodore R. McKeldin dedicates John Hanson Highway that will eventually link Annapolis with Washington, D.C.

1958

November 23: The Colonial Ball, a celebration of the 250th anniversary of Annapolis' city charter, held in the State House.

1959

May 26: Navy–Marine Corps Memorial Stadium on Taylor Avenue dedicated.

August: Mayor's Committee on Off-Street Parking embraces a plan to move or demolish the Market House to make room for more parking. Another suggestion recommends that City Dock be filled in as a parking area.

1960

U. S. Naval Academy land size increases; 54.4 acres of land added by filling areas of Severn River and Spa Creek to create Dewey Field and a new Farragut Field.

1962

U. S. Route 50, the John Hanson Highway, opened all the way to Washington, D.C.

1965

July 21: St. Martin's Lutheran Church on Francis Street demolished to make way for a modern office building. Congregation moves to new building on Spa Road and Forest Drive.

October: Carvel Hall Hotel torn down. Restoration of William Paca House and Garden begins.

Then Again...*Annapolis, 1900–1965*

Annapolis, Maryland's capital city, the seat
of government for Anne Arundel County,
and home of the U. S. Naval Academy,
c. 1939. MdHR 2140–225

NOTE: *Addresses given in captions reflect present-day street numbers and names.*

Main Street, *left*, viewed from the second floor window of 205 Main Street, looking toward St. Anne's Church, 1899.
MdHR G 2140–33

Main Street, *right*, looking toward City Dock, 1899. The building under construction was Gottlieb's Department Store at 184–186 Main. At its left, with awnings at every window, is the Chesapeake House Hotel, which was torn down c. 1923 to make way for a Woolworth's five-and-dime store.
MdHR G 2140–34

"I owe the town a debt because they were just terrific. Walking down Main Street was like being a star of a play. You just felt like you were a star. You walked down Main Street and everybody knew you in a short time. Very friendly, very kindly town.

Everything took place on Main Street. Parsons was the most wonderful store in the world. Down in the basement you could buy curtains and mattresses and oil cloth, and upstairs you bought your daughter's winter coat, leggings, and a hat. And the ribbon counter! The ribbon counter at Parson's and the buttons and the trimmings and the lace was just something unbelievable.

On Main Street there was a grocery store where you sat at the counter. You said, 'Hi, Joe.'

'How you doing, Miss? What can I do for you today?'

'Well, I'd like a piece of that nice cheese.' You sat at the counter, and he would go get the cheese. You didn't go around picking anything up. It was an old-fashioned grocery store where he stood with an apron on.

And there were two greengrocers. One woman would have such a nerve. She would sell the oldest stuff you ever saw. 'You don't like them? You don't like?' It was terrible stuff.

And there was one down the street that was a lovely big Italian store. That was where you went if you wanted real lasagna dough and if you wanted real ricotta cheese. If you wanted those things, you'd have to go in there and order them. But that's where you could get stuff to make real Italian food." [1]

"Every store had an iron-pipe canvas shade that came down. The awnings weren't like the ones you rolled down that came halfway and hung out. You had big round pipes, black pipes, that came out of the curb on the sidewalk, straight up, and right-angled to the building, screwed to the building. Then they had a white canvas awning that rolled down on big wooden poles and was controlled by cord, heavy clothesline cord, that tied to the side of the building. That's how you let your awning down. We used them year-round. You had to protect the merchandise displayed in your window." [2]

"My grandfather, in later years, was in the old city fish market that they had at the dock. There was a framed fish market with stalls on piles over the water. They tore that down in 1930. At one end of the fish market there was a colored restaurant. The man who ran the colored restaurant was a man named George Cromwell. That was for colored people. On the other end of the fish market there was a restaurant for white people. They called them cook shops.

We had a colored man that worked for my father, that clerked for my father, in the grocery business out here on Dock Street, who used to send me over to the cook shop at lunchtime. He had a tin pail. You could get a nice big tin pail filled up with black-eyed peas for fifteen cents or get a great big hardhead split, laid open, fried, for fifteen cents, with two pieces of bread. George Cromwell ran the cook shop on a big coal stove, wood and coal stove, in the back of his restaurant. Around about eleven o'clock or so, he would start frying his fish, great big hardheads in these big skillets, and he'd pile them up on a shelf in back of the stove on big plates, and he'd store them up so when people came in, he could just warm them up and he'd have it so when fifteen or twenty people came in and they all wanted fish at the same time, he'd serve them right away.

The cockroaches just covered the fish! Cockroaches everyplace! Never hurt anybody. They might have even eaten a few cockroaches. Who knows? But the cockroaches were running all over the place and nobody paid any attention to it.

I used to collect shoe boxes. They packed soft crabs in shoe boxes. So we would go around all the shoe stores in Annapolis with our wagons and get shoe boxes. The people who owned the fish market stalls would buy them from us for a penny apiece. That's how we made our movie money and our pocket money, by selling newspapers and shoe boxes to the people who had the stalls in the old fish market.

They tore that market down there in 1930, as I said. I was only ten years old. I was ten years old, into my eleventh year. Walter Quenstedt, who was a Republican, and my grandfather was a Republican, my grandfather probably gave him his biggest contribution in 1929, when he was running for election. He gave him one hundred dollars. Walter Quenstedt promised my grandfather that they would tear the old market down and build a new market right where it was. Well, they tore the old market down, but they didn't rebuild where it was. They outfitted the present city market in stalls and installed ice boxes, and they had to move across the street." [3]

The opening of Gottlieb's, Annapolis' first department store, at 184–186 Main Street in October 1899 was a newsworthy occasion in Annapolis. The *Evening Capital* reported that three to four thousand people attended the event where the Naval Academy band gave a concert. MdHR G 2140–350

"Gottlieb's was a department store, and the thing that fascinated me were those little pneumatic things that had a little collar on them, and you put the money in there and then 'whoosh' and they'd go on up. They had the office between the first and second floor, and they'd make the change, send it on back. It's just something that today nobody ever pays attention to. You go to the bank, a drive-in bank, and you put money in, and it disappears. That was in the open in Gottlieb's store, and it was a wonderful thing to see." [4]

"We formed the Young Cosmopolitan Club of Annapolis and Anne Arundel County, and one of our first acts was to assist Historic Annapolis in the display of the Carroll, Barrister House, prior to its moving, when it was still on the corner of Conduit and Main Street. This is the first thing that HA did. They were looking for people who would serve as hostesses in the house. We were maybe seniors in high school, or juniors.

We spent several weekends in the Carroll, Barrister House telling just totally untutored lies to people who came through. They were raising money to move the house. And we just said terrible things. Here were all of these sixteen-year-old girls being hostesses, not doing a particularly good job, but we were feeling very proud of ourselves. We were doing something for the community, and everybody's boyfriend had to come, and midshipmen would stop in and, of course, all the old people who were interested in the house and were being told awful stories. Nobody had primed us, but HA was very appreciative.

I remember standing in the library, the paneled library of the Carroll, Barrister House, and saying, 'Notice the paneling,' in very weighty tones. I remember knowing nothing, nothing, and making up some story about the paneling in this house and telling stories about the family—they weren't true. We giggled a lot. It was fun." [6]

"Woolworth's was where the Chesapeake House had been. That was a hotel, and I have a real faint memory of watching a human spider walk up the side of the Chesapeake House. We stood over by the Republic Theatre and watched this guy. Surely he had a rope, but it was a real daring feat to walk up the side of the building. They called him the human spider." [5]

Chesapeake House, *above*, c. 1898, was located on the site of 188 Main Street. Once a popular hotel and saloon, it was demolished during Prohibition. MdHR G 1890–632

Right, Carroll the Barrister House on its original site at the corner of Main and Conduit streets, c. 1900. In 1955, the house was moved to St. John's College campus. MdHR G 182–1290

Annapolis High School Class of 1901. MdHR G 2140–25

"We walked to Green Street school. Every day there was a whole contingent of kids, because there were loads of kids around our neighborhood, and every day we walked to school and walked home for lunch and then walked back. There was no cafeteria. As I remember it, the kids who lived in Davidsonville and the country brought their lunches, and they would all eat in a room. But the walkers went home. And I often now think to myself, How did we do it? We had an hour and walked home." [7]

Students at Annapolis Grammar School posed there in May 1901. The public elementary and high schools for white children were adjacent to each other on Green Street. MdHR G 2140–24

Thomas Point Gunning Club, *left*, 1903.
MdHR G 2140–320

Below, members of the Gates family posed in their parlor in 1902. MdHR G 2140–365

"So it was very much a situation where the children were to be seen and not heard, and I was a very polite little boy and I was allowed to stay in with the menfolk while they had their cigars or pipes after dinner. The ladies would usually repair to the parlor and the men would sit in their room and they would dust off these old military yarns or Indian adventures. Doc Snyder would come from time to time and he had been an Indian fighter on the frontier against the Sioux and the Cheyenne. And here I was, I wasn't reading any of this in history books, I was listening to it, you know, from the horse's mouth, so to speak." [8]

"I remember the good times we had and the fun in the evenings playing all sorts of games, sometimes card games and sometimes word games, all sorts of games that can be played by a group without any radio or television or anything like that. And we sang a lot, all ages, and without accompaniment. My father and mother knew a great many songs. And they would sort of lead the way for us, and we'd sing along and learn the songs ultimately ourselves. And we just had many, many evenings there when we would just sing and sing and sing, and I thought it was lots of fun." [9]

By the end of 1904, the dome of the new Naval Academy chapel was almost complete. Practically all of the work was done by means of hanging scaffolds. As the work progressed, the lower scaffolds were removed and added to the top, a new construction technique. MdHR G 2140–334

"Everything was torn down, and the Naval Academy was completely rebuilt at the turn of the century. The only thing left standing was a monument or two. The only buildings standing were the two guard houses at either side of the Maryland Avenue gate." [10]

Construction of the new dormitory for midshipmen at the Naval Academy was in its early stages on May 12, 1902, when the photograph *at right* was taken. Later additions eventually made Bancroft Hall the largest dormitory in the world. MdHR G 2140–332

NO. 53
MAY-12-02-2:30-P.M.

John R. Sherwood posed in one of Annapolis' first automobiles in front of Chaney's Storage at the corner of West Street and Colonial Avenue, c. 1904. MdHR G 2140–85A

The front porch was a cool and comfortable gathering place on hot summer days and nights. This house has changed greatly in appearance, but still stands at 114 Prince George Street. MdHR G 2140–176

"My father was offered a ride in the first automobile to come to Annapolis. A good friend of his, who was probably one of the richest men in town, invited him to ride out in his car. So we were very tickled when my father came back, and we said 'Well, what did you think? How did you like it?'

'Oh,' he said, 'it's just like sitting over a tea kettle.'" [11]

"One of the things I remember—and, of course, I'm telling you these things through the eyes of a child because everything seemed so enormous and so big in those days. But the thing I remember is that in the evening the grownups would come out on the porches, and they would sit around and they'd rock and swing or whatever they did in those days. They'd carry on conversations with each other sitting on their porches. My grandmother would be sitting there on the porch rocking away, and she'd be talking to the lady across the street or next door. And it was quiet enough. You didn't have the traffic, and the only noise was the kids playing.

The street was a playground. There were no cars. The few people that owned cars on the street had garages that they kept them in, and so the street became a playground. I mean, we played ball, we ran races, we did everything that you could think of in the street and didn't have to worry about traffic." [12]

14

Boucher's, c. 1905, was located at the foot of Market Street. Many Annapolitans stored their own canoes there or rented from Mr. Boucher. MdHR G 2140–96A

"Opposite Duvall Creek or Wells Cove was Boucher's, which had a boathouse, and they rented canoes. They had about fifty or sixty or maybe more canoes that they'd rent out, and the midshipmen would rent them on the weekends and they'd take their dates canoeing. They only had to canoe a few blocks and they were in virgin territory. So it was a very lovely area, very easy for them. They couldn't use automobiles, so they went paddling every weekend, you know, with their dates and had nature walks and just had a big time." [13]

"A bunch of the men were in the office part of the Boucher's canoe place one day in the summertime and it was thunderstorming. They all would sit around the potbelly stove in the wintertime and then in the summertime they just had the door open and they would dump their cigars and pipe ashes and everything in there. And this big thunderstorm came up and lightning hit a tree or hit the street about halfway up the hill. This ball of fire came bouncing down the hill—they said it was about the size of a basketball. And the men watched it coming, and it kept bouncing along the ground coming closer and closer and it came right through the door. And it went in the open door of the stove and sort of exploded, and the lid from the top went up and hit the ceiling and the men all scattered. And I heard about that for years. Nobody was hurt, but everybody was scared." [14]

16

In 1908, E. Everett Taylor, Louis Williams, Frank Alton, and Jake Meiser, a telephone installation crew, paused from their work on Main Street to face the camera.
MdHR G 2140–307

"I worked every summer from the time I was fourteen. I've always worked two jobs, even now. I worked at Admiral Laundry as a bag boy. I worked for Heidler Plumbing as a plumber's helper and dug ditches. I worked construction; I repaired lawn mowers. I've always worked. My father didn't make me, but he insisted that I find something to do in the summer to earn my money. I'm real glad he did that. I've worked ever since I was fourteen. I ought to have one hell of a Social Security when I'm ready." [15]

The corner of Main and Conduit streets appears behind these firefighters from Independent Fire Company No. 2, c. 1905–1909.
MdHR G 2140–302A

"My father was a fireman. In those days the fire truck was pulled by horses and had a big, huge canister of water—they toted it, the water. We had the firehouse up here on Duke of Gloucester Street. And the sirens would go off. And he would get up right away, no matter what, and go find out about the fire. He'd make a telephone call and find out.

But this time he ran out. And we were all awakened because the siren was going on and on and on and on. And so we went in the front bedroom. And my mother, I'll never forget her saying, 'My dear Lord, one could read a newspaper.' And you could. It was that bright. And it was all of Main Street—all those wooden houses, wooden stores—everything was burned." [16]

Nason's Tavern, 139 Dock Street, c. 1908. MdHR G 2140–299

"Fights were what brought on Prohibition, fights in Hell Point and around at the bars. The men would get paid cash. And they would get paid on Saturday night. Sunday's coming up, you know. They'd stop by, and there's some guy says, 'Joe, let's go and have a beer,' you know, 'Let's have a drink.' They'd get in there, and some people are just weak enough that, well, one person has to buy a drink and another one buys a drink. And they didn't get home with the money, and there would be a family that didn't have anything for that week. And the kids would have to go out and catch fish or catch crabs.

There were any number of people around Annapolis that, when they grew up, wouldn't touch a fish or a crab or an oyster because they had had to eat it when there was nothing else to eat. One of the ways to insult a kid on the playlot, especially those from Eastport, was to say, 'You eat fish,' denoting that they were so poor that they couldn't buy real food. Some of it was, of course, the times and the lack of jobs and work, because, you know, nothing was going on in Annapolis for many years. Nothing was going on, other than the Naval Academy, and St. John's, the post office. Where would you get a job? Taking in each other's wash? And, of course, there were the poor whites and then the black people, and they just had to make out one way or another." [17]

From 1908 to 1935, trolleys of the Washington, Baltimore & Annapolis electric line traveled the streets of Annapolis. The car *below* was on King George Street near Carvel Hall Hotel. MdHR G 2140–249

Horse-drawn vehicles like this one on State Circle near School Street were seen on Annapolis streets well into the twentieth century. MdHR G 2140–136

"I remember the WB&A—the cars went up West Street and around Church Circle and down Main Street. They went down to the King George Street wharf. The trains used to wake us up on South Street as they came around the circle at night.

The train that ran to Baltimore or Washington was the same that came around the circle and went down Main Street to the ferry. If you were going across on the ferry you got off there. They brought in a lot of people, particularly around June Week. Carvel Hall got its share, and that was a way we used to earn a little money, carrying bags for people. We would wait down there by Carvel Hall and when the train came in,

they would get off and if they needed a porter, we earned a little change.

We went to Baltimore occasionally at Christmastime. Of course, saying 'going to Baltimore' was just like saying 'going to Europe.' It was a distant place." [18]

"When I got my driver's license, garbage collection was done in a horse and buggy. That's how long I've had my license. I can still remember going around State Circle the day that I got my license, having to wait until the horse and wagon pulled over. They were collecting trash." [19]

21

Market Space, seen *at left* c. 1910, was the focus of much of the city's commercial life. During the growing season, the area often filled up with vendors hawking fresh seafood, vegetables, and flowers. MdHR G 2140–137

As was the custom of many families in business, the Rolnicks, who sold antique furniture, lived above their store at 99 Main Street. MdHR G 2140–129A

"I can remember the horses that people used to tie to hitching posts in front of the stores in town here. On a Saturday, when Saturday was a marketing day, all down around the docks and all you'd see these horses and buggies that would come in with the country folks. The folks that used to come from Edgewater used to sell flowers. They'd bring their cars and just sort of back them up and unload the flowers off of there. The people that had vegetables, they would just come in there, and some of them had cars and some of them had buggies.

It was a whole different feeling in those days. I run into you on the street today—'Oh, it's nice seeing you, Jack,' and how's this, and how's that. But, two minutes later, it's 'Nice talking to you, but I've got to go.' There's nothing that's important enough to stay an extra two minutes and have a conversation with a person about something." [20]

"I was born on Green Street and it was an area that was strictly divided. At the top part of the street you had mostly professional people, professors, teachers. And the lower part you had, more or less, the working members of the city. And, of course, the street was dominated by the Annapolis Grammar School and the Annapolis High School. At the lower part was a little general store and on the other corner was a bar. And down at the end of the street, you had a little park that we called Dog Turd Park." [21]

"Every Sunday, Mom would dress us up. Of course, back in those days, your dress-up dress had to be organdy. We had all colors of organdy dresses, because my uncle had an upholstery business, and his wife used to go buy organdy from Parsons and could stitch up a dress, just like that. So every Sunday we went down to the academy. That was our Sunday walk. We all would be dolled up. You didn't go down there looking any kind of way on a Sunday. We always got compliments on the way we looked." [22]

"The Stevens' house on Madison Place, that was like the public library. There was no public library in my early years. Some of my cousins had grown up and gone away, but they left a legacy of books, adventure stories and things like the western, *Trail of the Lonesome Pine.*

You could go in the front sitting room, and the door was always open because, you know, there were kids going in and out all the time and nobody could tell whose kids they were. So the Carricks would be there and maybe the Chambers, the Halls, the Gateses, the Martins, and the Eckens, all those kids would be in one time or another. And you'd go in and it would be sort of half-dark in there, only one front window as I remember—maybe there was two front windows. There'd be somebody in a chair like that with a book stuck up in front of him, and they wouldn't even look at you. You know, you could go in and out, and

The Gessner family at home at 5 Hill Street, c. 1910. MdHR G 2140–360

there would be somebody in their family or somebody in somebody else's family.

The ground out in the Stevens' backyard was so beat down that not a blade of grass grew around the house. It was packed down like clay in a tennis court. There was a hole in the back fence that you could crawl through to get the ball when you

knocked it over into Mr. Munroe's property. From where John Franklin Stevens built his house down to the railroad bank, there were no houses. It was a field, and that was our playground. There was a path that went across that and went down the hill, because a lot of people used to take the shortcut down the railroad track to get downtown." [23]

For many years, the majority of blacks in Annapolis were employed in service positions. *Above*, the staff at the Peggy Stewart Inn, 217 Hanover Street, posed for a group portrait c. 1915. MdHR G 2140–282

"My mother always had to work. My father died when I was young. There were seven of us; I was the youngest. My sisters and brothers helped take care of me. So you were told and trained to do certain things for your own good.

Mother had to be on the job at certain times in the morning until, maybe, late in the evenings. So we had to learn to take care of each other and do for ourselves. I guess it sort of brings you up to be self-sufficient and you just do it automat-ically. If you've got a strong parent that tells you to live this way, then this is the way you learn to live. And you do it; you have to. Just as simple as that.

She was gone from seven o'clock in the morning until eight o'clock at night, sometimes. So your sister was your mother until your mother came home. You'd do what she says and you'd do it the way she says do it, and she does it just like your mother would do it if she was there. And that's the way it is." [24]

Students at St. Mary's parochial school, first and second grades, November 1911. St. Mary's operated two schools, one for white children, one for black. Many black children who lived downtown attended St. Mary's regardless of whether or not they were Catholic. MdHR G 2140–294

"I went to St. Mary's school. I remember looking over the high board fence and there was a little colored school right next to St. Mary's parochial school, where Taylor's is. There was a little colored school. And the white nuns took care of them. And I looked over the fence one day and I looked at a little girl who was as white as I was. And I came home and told my mother.

And she said, 'Well, dear, perhaps it's what they call a mixed marriage.' I didn't know what that was, but I just accepted it. That's why she was there. Because I said, 'She looked just like me.' And she really did." [25]

"Eddie was always such a good big brother. He taught all of us how to swim. I remember his taking us down to what is now the Annapolis Yacht Club. That's where we all learned to swim, at the float down there. My brother would take us down, and I can remember Eddie throwing three of us over in the deep water at the same time. I had never taken a stroke in my life. And I'm coming gulping up, and he said to me, 'Sink or swim.' I think I was

seven or eight then. And I hear about kids having traumas all their life, and hating swimming because of an experience like that. Well, I don't know, it worked the opposite with us. We were all little fish all our lives and we loved it. When the spring came we would break through the ice to go swimming, to be the first one in.

We always had one or two canoes in the backyard. When my sister Frankie came home, she brought a

kayak with her from Honolulu. She'd been living in Hawaii, because her husband was navy. And she brought her kayak home. Every afternoon, the six girls in the family, the six youngest of the ten, we would go out in the kayak and canoe, and our greatest feat was to see how close we could get to the bow of the ferry that was crossing. Whoever could reach up and touch the bow, that person was sort of 'it' for the day. The captains of those

Skeleton Club of Annapolis, *left*, rowing on Spa Creek in 1914. Until the 1930s, when the yachting industry developed, most boats in local waters were workboats or canoes. MdHR G 2140–68A

The second bridge to Eastport, pictured *below* in 1916, opened to traffic in June 1907. Like its predecessor, it soon fell into disrepair. MdHR G 1890–6774

ferry boats, they hated, they couldn't stand us. They tried to kill us because they were so sick of us. Every day we would come out and try to cross, we would say, 'Now we're going to cross their bow.' And we did that for just ages. Then we would go and take our kayak and canoe out into the Bay. We would turn them over and go swimming all out in the Bay by ourselves, six girls." [26]

"If you were an Annapolitan, you didn't go over to Eastport. There was usually a group of young men on the other end of the bridge and the chances were they'd throw you into the creek if you went over there. By the same token, if an Eastporter came over to Annapolis, there was often a group of boys on the Annapolis side and they would return the compliment. So it just went on for years and you had your

own little neighborhoods. On a scale of toughness, the Hell Point boys rated a ten, and the Eastport boys rated about an eight. And the Slippery Hill boys, where I grew up, rated about three. So there was no contest." [27]

"I think Annapolis is southern enough to where I think we felt very close to our black population. We never had any money, but we would have someone when my mother wasn't well. And there was no such thing as a washing machine or anything then. I remember we had a preacher's wife when we were little, teeny kids. Her name was Mamie Barksdale. She had a sister, Martha. They would come and wash on Monday—one would come. If one couldn't come, the other would. And Mamie or Martha would come and wash on Monday and come and iron on Tuesday. That was the help that we had.

In Annapolis, black domestics were like part of the family. As they aged, they would bring in a daughter or a granddaughter who would do the running around the house. But the people let their older black people stay on as cooks or something. They would find a spot for them because they realized that they needed that, they needed the money. It was a very loving relationship between the white and the black people in the Annapolis area, which I think is a little bit of a hangover from slave days in a way that the good people loved them as part of their family." [28]

Many white children in Annapolis were raised in part by black nannies or nurse-maids. *Below*, Blanche Butler poses with her charges, Virginia and Raymond Rayhart, c. 1916. MdHR G 2140–381

"There was a wharf where the steamboats came in. Right down at the foot of Prince George Street. It was the Tolchester Company. The Tolchester boat used to come in and they'd pick up all the animals and vegetables and one thing or another, and they'd bring them all up Prince George Street. Cows, horses, whatever they were getting, pigs, everything came up the street. One cow got loose one day, and they had a terrible time, but they caught it. I always loved to go down to the wharf." [29]

During the night of August 4, 1915, the worst storm in history hit Annapolis. This was the scene the next day on lower Prince George Street. MdHR G 2140–389

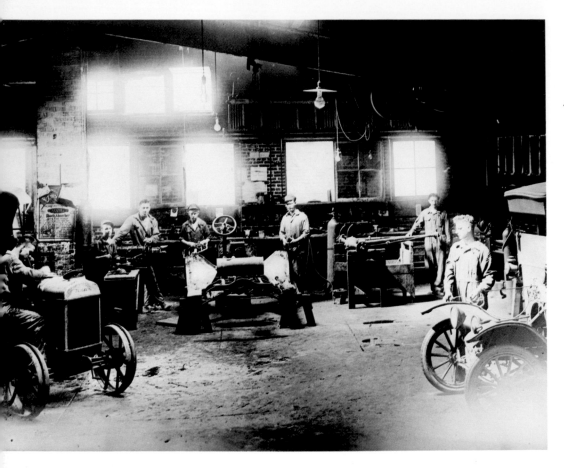

"You don't have the personal associations, either through school or church, as you did in those days. The people you dealt with were people that you went to school with, people that you played with as kids, people that were your business associates, employees, employers, people you went to church with. Anybody that wasn't born here, my grandmother called a squatter. We've got so many squatters around that they don't care. You don't have the individual merchants; you have shopping centers. You have clerks. You don't have mechanics working on your car; you have parts exchangers. You just don't have the personal touch that you used to." [30]

"My grandfather Gates' blacksmith shop was right next door to the house. Uncle Jack was a blacksmith, too. Automobiles had come in and he knew the horses were doomed, and he didn't want to do any other blacksmithing than being a farrier. He didn't want to do wagon work and all that sort of thing.

A blacksmith's shop was a shed made of boards, unpainted, generally oak boards. A good, substantial building, but it looked ramshackle. But the front of it would open, and stay open, and only in real cold

weather did they ever close the doors. One reason was that they had an open fire.

You made a coal fire—soft coal—and had a bellows that you either worked by hand or with a foot pedal to bring air in to bring that coal up to its highest heat. They made horseshoes various sizes, but to fit them to a horse's foot you had to put them in and bring them to a yellow heat, past red-hot, just getting toward a white-hot. And then you put them on the forge, and the forge was shaped so that you could

put the shoes over it and make them narrower by beating on them, or you could make them wider by stretching them over the anvil.

And then, in wet and snowy weather and icy weather, they had to put cleats on them. And that was when the blacksmith was very busy, because the horses had to have cleats on their shoes to be able to stand up on bricks and cobblestones and that sort of thing. They would take the shoes and get the back end of them hot and put them on the edge of the anvil and beat them

Jack Gates, seen *above* c. 1915, maintained a blacksmith shop on West Street at today's Russell Street intersection. MdHR G 2140–358

down so that it made a sharp cleat on the back end. Then they took a small piece of iron that they cut off of a bar—white-hot—and welded it to the front of the shoe to give it a front cleat, and then it had two cleats in back and one in front.

It was generally a one-man operation, but people gathered there to watch him work, to converse, and there would be people waiting." [31]

"Rookie was a local boy, and the people just liked him. He had customers follow him all over Annapolis. At A&P we had Louis Jones, Mickey Gates, James Patterson, and Eddie Ford—these are all meat cutters that used to be in Annapolis. They had their own customers. People are critical when it comes to meat." [32]

Before the advent of the supermarket and pre-packaged food, women did their grocery shopping on a daily basis. Neighborhood stores provided the basics, but meats were usually purchased from butcher shops like Benjamin Britton's at 77 West Street. Here, Mr. Britton displays his wares in 1914. In later years, he carried more groceries.
MdHR G 2140–253

From its opening in 1902, the Colonial Theatre had provided Annapolis' most elegant setting for stage and screen productions. MdHR G 2140–173A

"In 1919, my younger brother had just arrived, and a sister older than I had pneumonia. Mother had the flu. That night, about midnight, the telephone rang. We had a nurse taking care of all of these sick people and she answered the telephone and called my father. We asked what was going on. I was seven years old and Kitty was four years old.

She said, 'Everything is all right, but there is a fire. Just be quiet and

The fire that destroyed the Colonial Theatre on Conduit Street on January 17, 1919, also damaged several businesses, including Strange & White around the corner at 155–157 Main Street. MdHR G 2140–392

I'll show it to you. You're going to be all right.' We had little shirtwaist boxes in front of each window in the bedroom. She put one of us on each one and put a blanket around us and showed us the fire. The fire started in the Colonial Theatre, which was owned by my uncle. It started in the screen in the back, and it spread to the stores on Main Street, to Dr. Feldmeyer's drug store, to my grandfather's paint and wallpaper shop, and to Strange & White clothing store.

And I can still remember, Kitty and I started to cry. Kitty kept saying, 'We're going to starve, we're going to starve!'" [33]

"My first recollection of the Colonial Theatre is when it was in rubbles after the fire. I remember the fire, but we didn't go. We knew it was something terrible because the whole place was lighted up. We could actually see right through to the fire from the middle of Market Street right on up. I was six years old. You just didn't take kids to fires. I remember standing there at the window and ahhing and oohing. I think that the Tilghmans and the Trautweins were even considering moving out. It looked so bad at the time from where we were on Market Street. It was a bad fire." [34]

Local physician J. Oliver Purvis, Sr. was a captain in the medical corps during World War I. MdHR G 2258–14

"When the war was over, they had a parade for Company M. There were these two brothers. One was a pilot, and when he was learning to fly, it was against regulations, against the law, to buzz Annapolis. But he would buzz the State House just to let his mother know he was still alive. And he was sort of a hero. He had a brother who stayed around Annapolis, and he was quite a character. He had lots of navy wives who were left alone that he took care of.

Anyhow, the parade came down West Street, and I was on Church Circle on the church side on the sidewalk. The WB&A train, at that time, came down West Street, came around the right side of the circle, and went down Main Street. These brothers were out in front of Company M, and they were drunker than lords. They had pulled their shirts off, and they were, you know, sort of half bare-chested and they were staggering from one side of the street to the other. And the train came down West Street, and Company M split, you know. The officers gave the order and they split on each side. And the car came down, and the brothers were just weaving back and forth across in front of it. Weaving back and forth, and it took about twenty to twenty-five minutes for the parade to get past Church Circle. And that's what I remember about it. The whole parade had to wait, you know, for this car to go by. And the car

"My father was in the army, and he was down in Chattanooga, Tennessee, learning to drill as an army officer. And people in Annapolis were dying like flies from the flu epidemic in 1918. Almost all the doctors were gone. The undertakers couldn't keep up with it and Mother would write Daddy these gloomy letters how everything was so bad, and he was depressed. And then he'd get a letter from me. 'Oh, everything is fine, everybody is all right.' I was only eight years old." [35]

couldn't go by because these guys were just staggering around and falling all over the place. The Naval Academy band led the parade. They were probably down by the dock waiting for the rest of the parade.

At that time, Piney Lowman was the only policeman on duty in the daytime in Annapolis, and I don't know where he was. There was nobody to get these guys, and nobody wanted to interfere with them, you know. First place, they were both dangerous because they were fighters and it was known, and you didn't tamper with them because you might get slugged in the jaw or whatever, because they were drunk. So they just went on and went on down Main Street. And the car could only go as fast as they did.

The other soldiers were having a good time because they were talking to everybody along the way, all their friends and relatives. It made it better for them, to tell you the truth.

Veterans of "the war to end all wars" returned triumphantly to Annapolis in 1919, and many of them gathered for this group portrait on the steps of the State House. MdHR G 2140–234

Rather than just marching, they could sort of break ranks and talk. They were just standing there and talking and joking and going on. Maybe there was a drink or two passed around, too, I don't know, but I didn't see that." [36]

"My four cousins—they were all girls—and I played together all up and down Green Street, Fleet Street, Cornhill Street. We used to go into McCready's and get all of his discarded boxes and we would drag them into our backyard and we would make dollhouses—we would make them so good, until actually we could stay out in them in the rain. One day my grandmother came home all excited and upset—it was pouring rain—and she was looking for her girls. And we were comfortable out in our dollhouse sound asleep." [37]

"Annapolis has always been a town of newcomers. Now, I think at the same time, the people who ran Annapolis, the people who sat on city council, may have been the only natives. The natives ran the town politically. They were the firemen, they were the policemen, they were the civil servants. In that sense, the place where I was most treated as an outsider was in City Hall. As for the community, outside the government, I was just like everybody else, just arrived." [38]

McCready's furniture store, 2–4 Francis Street, was just down the street from the headquarters of the Improved Order of Red Men, 1919. MdHR G 2140–471

41

Steamboats were regular visitors at the Prince George Street wharf, *below*. There was another wharf at the foot of King George Street for ferries to the Eastern Shore.
MdHR G 2140–3A

Water transport conveyed Annapolitans to and from Baltimore and the river landings and delivered food and livestock to city markets and slaughterhouses.
MdHR G 2140–20A

"This guy Johnson taught me and my brother how to dive for nickels and dimes when the ferries came in. During the late thirties and early forties, you could get out in that water and bring home twelve dollars a day. Your father and mother wasn't making no more than three bucks a week, you know.

The ferryboat would come in to the dock, then they would load the people, the cars and the passengers. Well, the passengers came in first. The people would get out of their cars, and then they would go up to the upper decks and look over at the harbor. And when they looked down, there we were, three of us, four or five. And somebody would say, 'Hey, Mama. Hey, look at that little guy down there. What is he

doing?' Then my brother would holler, 'Throw a nickel! Throw a quarter! Throw a dime!'

And in the water, whether you know it or not, a dime looks like the size of a quarter. A nickel looks like the size of a half dollar. A quarter looks like the size of a silver dollar, because it magnifies in water. And when you throw a coin in water, it just doesn't go right down and sink. It sort of drops like a leaf out of a tree. Zip, zip, zip, zip. It slows up.

You would stick them in your mouth. And I think I swallowed about eleven cents in my life. Thank God no trouble, you know, on the exit end. Then we would swim on to shore, and we would take it all out, and we'd count it up. Then we'd wait for the next boat." [39]

"We used to have what you'd call a family boat excursion every year that left from down at the City Dock, and we'd go to Cambridge. And that was a family picnic, all day long. And your folks cooked all night long or a couple days to prepare stuff to go on that boat. In fact, the entire black community was gone on that boat. And talk about the good time we'd have! Music and, oh, just good times.

I'm telling you I'm talking about

just about the entire black community! The families went and they took their food. All kinds of good eating. You could eat from just about anybody on the boat, you know. It was really something. I often said, I said, 'God, they could burn the whole black community down while we're gone.' It was terrific. We were down here every year for that. We came to Annapolis for that.

One year my two grandmothers cooked, cooked, cooked all night long. And then the payoff was Mr. Brewer, that was my grandmother's second husband, didn't get the ticket for the rest of us. So there was my grandmothers, both of them, out on the dock. They couldn't get on, all that good food out there. I didn't have a ticket. But, man, guess what? Flora jumped on that boat and flew right up to the top deck, said, 'They won't find me.' And I looked over after I got up there and I knew I was safe. You know, nobody had noticed. I had made sure I sneaked on right over the side and right up to the top deck. And I looked down and my heart was hurt. My grandmothers sitting there and the boat pulling off and all that good food sitting there with them. It was enough to make you sick. I had no problems because, like I said, everybody fed everybody. And I had oodles of relatives on the boat. But I wanted that good food my grandmothers had fixed." [40]

During the early part of the twentieth century, middle and upper class women rarely worked outside the home. Many were involved in volunteer activities that expanded their social lives and provided services to the community. *At right*, Margaret Trautwein and Jo Hartman paused by the Trautwein family car on Market Street in the 1920s. MdHR G 2140–170

"The stores that were in Eastport at the time were Mr. Emory Bowen's store which was down on the corner of Chesapeake Avenue and Second Street, and then there was that little store the Rileys operated. That was a very small one-room grocery store. They were operating stores in their homes.

I lived a way out of Eastport proper, per se, and it was a distance, but then, in those days, you didn't consider it a distance. Today, if you go two blocks, you've gone a distance. But we really had a lot of these little tiny stores and if we needed something, oh, particularly difficult to find here, you went over to Main Street, and you got your butter, and your eggs, and what have you, fresh.

We really thought we were something else when we got the A&P store. We were big time." [41]

Eastport was a community separate from Annapolis until it was annexed by the city in 1951. Laid out in 1868, old Eastport extended from the Severn River to Sixth Street. By the time Jennie F. Riley and her daughter Bessie Wilson posed on Sixth Street, *at left* c. 1919, most Eastporters lived in small neat houses with a garden in the backyard. MdHR G 2140–150A

"In those days, many of those large homes were boarding homes because single women did not live alone. They didn't have apartments; there were no apartments. So single women and single men lived with other people in boardinghouses. That was very common, especially with teachers. You had breakfast and dinner in the boardinghouse.

They would take these boarders in, that was always so funny to me. People took in boarders in all those houses that belonged to modest people on Market Street and Union Street and all of those little streets. The husbands all worked as plumbers, electricians, or painters in the Naval Academy.

The wives took in girls, the midshipmen's girls, the drags. During June Week the family made sacrifices—they rented their own bedrooms. Sometimes they might even put a mattress on the kitchen table—and that's where they slept. But they paid off the houses. Every one of those houses! The wives earned the money, but they didn't go to work. There weren't many things for wives to do in those days and the wives stayed home.

These women who were sleeping on mattresses on top of their kitchen table, they had one strong desire if they had a daughter—to marry her off to a midshipman." [42]

45

"The best sleigh-riding was Conduit Street, Market Street and Revell Street. You had to have suicidal tendencies to sleigh-ride down Revell Street because that was the steepest hill of all. And, of course, nowadays when you look at the bottoms of the streets, there's a nice neat little bulkhead down there, which would stop you. But in those days, they just simply went right down into the creek. If you did not make the proper turn, you'd end up overboard or out on the ice. And I saw a fair number of injuries connected with that.

Sometimes the Hell Point boys would come over, because it's all flat down at Hell Point, there wasn't any real sleigh-riding. And although we weren't allowed to go to Hell Point, the Hell Pointers could go pretty well wherever they wanted."
[43]

"My mother drove a horse and buggy on Bay Ridge Avenue, which was oyster-shelled. Eastport was strictly country. You either walked wherever you were going or you did not get there—unless you had a horse and buggy.

Our part of Eastport was completely farmland. A man named Elliott sold us all milk. I would cross the field. I was five, and I would cross the field to go to his home and pick up my milk for my breakfast or what have you, whatever my mother needed." [44]

Florence Russell and Kadelia Shultz were content to sit on the porch at 113 Chesapeake Avenue in Eastport, c. 1917. MdHR G 2140–171

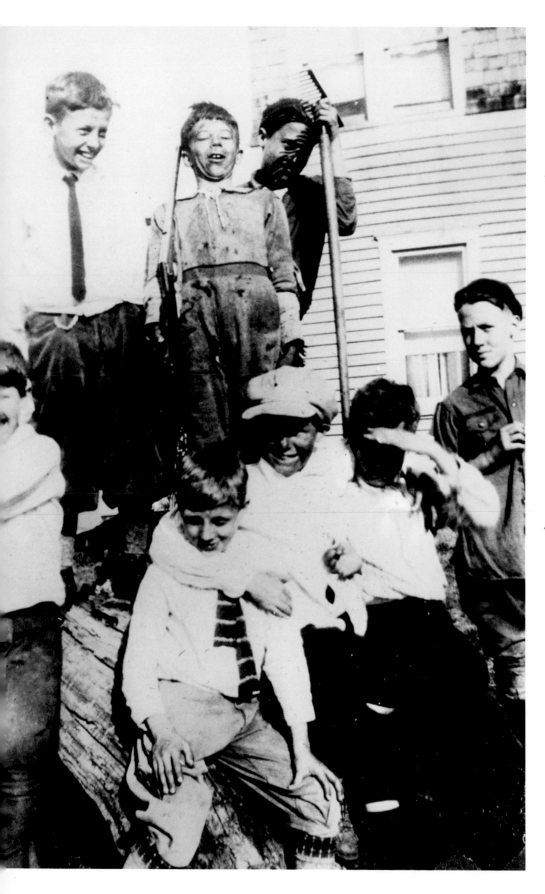

Neighborhood gangs were a way of life among the boys in Annapolis c. 1920, when this pack roamed the streets of Slippery Hill. MdHR G 2140–169

"The city had nothing in a way of organized programs for young people in comparison to what it's like today. We had groups, we had teams, but it was necessary for you to develop it. You and your friends would have to initiate the ideas, develop the programs, and in the case of sports, you had to subsidize your own interests. I mean, it wasn't any question of going someplace and being given something. And if you could create and develop your own fun it developed a lot of initiative from the guys, and the girls, too. So we would organize our own entertainment." [45]

OVERLEAF:

"In the summertime Annapolis emptied out. I knew several people who rented their houses in Annapolis to people who came here for the summer while they went to the Thousand Islands for their summer vacation.

There were even people who had houses in town and then summer places at Bay Ridge. Some even had summer places at Horn Point and a town house on Prince George. It was cool and you could go swimming—people didn't have cars as much." [46]

Following pages: Members of several prominent Annapolis families, the Feldmeyers, the Purvises, the Linthicums, the Mosses, and the Hills, joined this excursion to Horn Point c. 1921. MdHR G 2258–8

There were few restaurants in Annapolis—instead, people frequented tearooms or lunchcounters in drug stores, like this one in Gilbert's Pharmacy at the corner of State Circle and East Street, c. 1922.
MdHR G 1936–868

"Would you believe that for twenty-five cents I could get a fifteen-cent grilled-cheese sandwich, a five-cent bag of potato chips and a five-cent Coke, and that was lunch when I was working at the Circle Theatre. When I tell people that today, they don't believe it, but it's true.

Gilbert's was like a neighborhood pharmacy where they had good food. As you walked in the front, that's where all the drugs and the cosmetics were, and then you walked toward the back and there was a snack bar, with a soda fountain and tables, where you could go in and order sandwiches and soups.

It was a very busy place. I would say it was one of the most well-known drug stores in the city of Annapolis. Read's was a great high school hangout. The kids would go in there after school and they had jukeboxes. They'd get a fifteen-cent Coke and stay there all day long, which really made Read's mad because, when people wanted to come in, there'd be no place to sit." [47]

Sam Finkelstein operated a store in Parole on the western outskirts of Annapolis. Here, he stopped on Church Circle adjacent to the Governor's Mansion in the 1920s, before it was changed from its original Victorian architecture. MdHR G 2140–198

"You were in the country when you got to Camp Parole. Finkelstein, he had a junk store out there. He called it antiques, but I called it junk." [48]

52

Segregated schools were the norm in Annapolis, as elsewhere in Maryland, until the late 1950s. Stanton School was both elementary and high school in 1922 when the Elks' football team posed there. MdHR G 2010–50A

Baby Day, a tradition at Annapolis High School, was the occasion c. 1922 for an excursion up the Severn River where this photograph was taken. MdHR G 2140–363

"When we were growing up, we didn't have anything. We didn't have TVs and we didn't have money to go to the movies or stuff, so we had to play sports. What I got out of it is the camaraderie. You know, when you play a sport, particularly a team sport, you form a bond, not just with the people you play with, but with the people you play against. You learn respect, and you earn respect, too. That's something I always liked about it. People who recognize that you're really, you know, you're doing the best you can. You don't have to be the greatest athlete in the world, but people recognize the fact that, hey, you're hustling and doing the best you can. I think you earn respect, and I think sports gives that to you." [49]

"During the time that I was going to high school, there was no place to go for parties and dances other than Carvel Hall. The class ahead of us started a secret fraternity. And so we did the same thing, and we called ours 'The Blinking Buzzards.' I was secretary and treasurer. We threw dances down at Carvel Hall on Saturday nights.

Our money went to the athletic program. There was no such thing as athletic funds from the county or state or whatever. It was one dollar per person. It was stags and drags, and a lot of boys went. There weren't enough girls in Annapolis to go around, especially for Saturday nights. There was just a multiplicity of men around, and some of them with uniforms on, an extra added attraction. That was competition." [50]

In May 1923, the first class of nurses graduated from the local Emergency Hospital. Standing, left to right: Drs. Walton H. Hopkins, John T. Russell, J. Oliver Purvis, and James J. Murphy. Seated: Margaret Wohlgemuth, Helen Walrath, Dr. Frances E. Weitzman, Madaline Grimes, and Ada Leitch. MdHR G 2140–175

"Another one of my heroes was Dr. Purvis, old Dr. Purvis. I'm going back to Murray Avenue again. And this is when, believe it or not, doctors made house calls, for God's sake. When my grandparents were sick, they were sick at home. I remember that. You know, the hospital was just a fraction of the size it is today. But my grandparents were sick at home, and they died at home, and they were laid out at home when they died.

Dr. Purvis would come in the house, and he would do everything he could for my grandmother or grandfather, whoever he was attending at the time. He was just a caring person.

His house was on the corner of Shaw Street and Franklin. Nice old home, and his office was down in the basement. I can see him walking up Murray Avenue now with that little black bag in his hand.

Old Dr. Anderson was another one. His place was over on Southgate Avenue. I remember Dr. Anderson so well years later. I thought he was just a tremendous person. This was, of course, after I had gotten older and I was still active in athletic sports in Annapolis. I belonged to the Annapolis Athletic Association, and whenever we had broken bones, sprains, or contusions or anything else, we'd go see Dr. Anderson. He'd fix us up and never charge us a penny. He did everything free of charge. He was just a fantastic person." [51]

Madison Place was the dividing line for Annapolis school districts. Children from Madison Place attended elementary school on Green Street while those from Jefferson Street, one block west, attended Germantown School. *Above,* John Waliser Holman, Wallace Holman, and Dorothy Ford were ready to ride in 1923. MdHR G 2140–323

"At one time or another, everybody in Annapolis lived on Madison Place, honestly. My mother had very close friends who lived up at the end of Madison Place, Mr. and Mrs. Stevens—he was the postmaster for many years. In those days grocery stores stayed open until midnight on Saturday night. They opened at six o'clock in the morning and stayed open until midnight. Mr. Stevens and Mrs. Stevens would never let my mother stay alone there. They always, every Saturday night, would come and stay with her. I distinctly remember one day Mr. Stevens sweeping the pavement in front of the store and somebody going by and saying, 'Well, look at the postmaster sweeping Mrs. Levy's pavement.' It was almost like an extended family in that neighborhood." [52]

A State Roads Commission crew resurfaced West Street at Spa Road c. 1922, *at left*. At that time, the city limits were just a block away. MdHR G 1890–6753

The original bridge over the Severn River was wooden, *below*. Its replacement, which opened in 1924, was constructed of steel and concrete. MdHR G 2140–260

"Mostly everything was done by hand. I used to see men mix concrete with just shovels and water. They would just lay it out on a street, the sand, the gravel, then they'd put the dry powder concrete mix in there, and they would mix it together. One would get on each end, and they would meet each other in the middle. And then they would make a little valley in it, then they would pour in the water, and they would mix it all up before that water started rolling out of it. They were very good at it." [53]

"I worked on the old Severn River bridge. I graduated from high school in '23, and I was going to go to college that year, and I went over there and worked on the bridge as a laborer. I just went over and signed up, and they put me in with a crew of black people—very nice guys, they were. And I can remember that I was driving stakes—and I had

been playing football in high school and I felt pretty strong—but I was missing the stakes. And there was a nice colored guy who said, 'You don't need to throw that hammer.' He said, 'You just take it up and let the good Lord bring it down. You guide it.' It was a lesson that I have never forgotten—that it's not the force that you use, it's the accuracy; and I used that in my athletic career.

But after four or five days of working with that crew of these men who were supporting families and so on, I got to feeling pretty bad about it. I was getting thirty-five cents an hour for ten hours work a day and for six days a week, and I didn't know what I was doing. I was just going along with them, and some of these black guys really knew what they were doing. And there was one leader, and I'm sure he was getting only the same amount of money that I was." [54]

57

Most Annapolitans considered the Naval Academy a giant city park that almost always had some form of entertainment in progress. Band concerts, parades like this one c. 1925, and a wide range of sporting events kept the locals, as well as the midshipmen and faculty families, busy.
MdHR G 1936–1183

"It was a free and easy world. I had a nurse. One thing I remember very distinctly, the nursemaids all took the little children over to the Naval Academy, particularly around June Week when they'd have sham battles. The midshipmen would have

sham battles on the field over here which is no longer in existence, there's a building on it now, but it used to be, I guess it was called Farragut Field. And they used to play football and everything else there. And they had bleachers and we used to go over there and watch the sham battles. And the nursemaids would take us all over, and I would hide under the bleachers because they'd start shooting these big guns, and it used to scare me out of my wits." [55]

Many local boys attended St. John's College, both because it was convenient and because of the quality of its education. Since the nineteenth century, the college had offered military training as part of its curriculum, but in 1923, St. John's abolished compulsory military training for all students and changed its focus to the liberal arts. *Above,* the last ROTC unit trains with Major Enoch Garey in 1924. MdHR G 2140–374

"There were seven of us from Annapolis High School who went to St. John's in 1923. We had about 128, I think, when we entered, but we only finished with about twenty-seven. St. John's had been a military school, and Major Garey was hired to make it a civilian school, and he was determined to make it the best small college in the country.

The 'war to end wars' was over, and there was no need for military schools anymore. They were going to have students there who were students. They didn't have any supervision on the campus; you could do what you wanted to do. But you were supposed to be a gentleman. You were supposed to conduct yourself like a civilized human being, and when you didn't, you went out." [56]

St. John's College was respected widely for the athletic prowess of its teams. *Above*, the 1925 football team competed with Johns Hopkins at Homewood Field in Baltimore. MdHR G 2140–368

"St. John's was a pretty tough athletic school in those days. We played the small colleges around the area. Johns Hopkins was our mortal enemy, and we used to play them on Thanksgiving Day until it got out of style. And then we played the last game of the season with them. And we played Pennsylvania Military College, which was a long-standing thing because they were two military colleges. At times, we played the University of Virginia and Western Maryland and Mount St. Mary's and Gettysburg." [57]

Competition between the Naval Academy and St. John's was usually gentlemanly and usually centered on women. For a town of its size, Annapolis had an over-abundance of young men desirous of female company. Local and visiting girls often had to do double duty, attending dances at the academy in the early evening followed by fraternity parties at St. John's—a practice known as late dating. MdHR G 2140–370

"Late dating was very popular in my day. One of the stratagems was to send one boy down in a tuxedo to a navy hop to find some gal that he knew and find out how many girls were staying at the place where she was, because, you know, some of them were staying four and five to a room. One of our favorite girls was a red-headed girl by the name of Georgia Brown. She was a secretary in Baltimore, and she was what you'd call a navy widow, because she'd been around quite a while. But she was the sweetest little girl and danced just like a butterfly.

Georgia stayed in one of those houses down on King George Street across from the wall—they're still there in between Martin Street and Randall. We'd get Georgia to line up the girls at the house, and it would be, you know, like seven or eight or so. And then somebody else would line up some others. And I remember one time going down in my room. One of our favorite girls was a red-headed girl by the name of Ford at about 11:15, and the girls came pouring out of the house and jumped in. Just then a bunch of midshipmen came over the wall, and, boy, I put that old Ford into first gear and I roared out of there. They were 'Frenching' it, as they called it, you know, in the Naval Academy. They were taking French leave coming over the wall. They were coming out to join the girls who had taken off. That's where the animosity came in. They didn't mind it so much if they didn't know about it, but when they found out!" [58]

Fraternities were the center of most social life at St. John's during the late 1920s and early 1930s. In 1937, the college adopted a radical new program centered on the Great Books, and fraternities were abolished. MdHR G 1936–2539A

"At that time, I was in the KA fraternity, and we were in a house on St. John's Street. And we had a Victrola—well, anyhow, it was a great big phonograph. We didn't have any rugs on the floor so we just put some cornmeal down on the floor to make it slipperier and would have a dance and have some gin and whatever.

One time there was a midshipman at the Naval Academy who had been a KA at the University of Georgia before he went to the Naval Academy. Anderson was his name, and I couldn't tell you what his first name was because we called him Andy. But he had a star in his collar; he was a bright student. But he used to come out, and he had a roommate who was a big, dumb guard on the football team, and Andy's mission at the Naval Academy was to get this guard through school. The football player's job was to meet Andy at the Maryland Avenue gate, which was the main gate at that time. And so one of the guys would go down with Andy to the gate, holding on to his arm, and then he'd take hold of his roommate's arm and go down and stand inspection alongside of him.

Andy's father was a Prohibition administrator of the state of Georgia, and when Andy graduated and he came up for June Week, the chauffeur had gotten the word from Andy and he brought a keg of confiscated moonshine up in the back of the limousine. I don't know whether his father was aware of it being in there or not. He may have been. He may have been a party to it, I don't know. But that keg of hooch was put in the basement room there with a spigot in it, and we really had a party for a whole week." [59]

Murray Hill was subdivided in 1890 by George Melvin, who carved the land into lots that were placed on the market at two to four hundred dollars each. The Meredith family home at 38 Franklin Street is pictured *below* c. 1925. MdHR G 1936–1128

The development of Murray Hill was gradual. By 1918, about the time that the photograph *at right* was taken, the area behind Southgate Avenue was still an open field. MdHR G 2140–236A

"My parents moved to Southgate Avenue on New Year's Eve of 1924. It wasn't paved until after we moved out there. There was mud out front.

Behind us, there was open fields, which was the carnival and fairgrounds. It was known as Stehle's grounds. All the circuses came there and the largest one that ever came was Sparks Brothers, and they came on railroad cars and the whole outfit came all the way up behind our house. But that was the only one that was ever that big that came there. The fire department carnivals were held over there where Monticello Avenue comes off West Street.

Down where Stewart Avenue is, there was a spring. As kids, we used to go into the woods and across there over to Monticello Avenue, and the only way you could get across it was one log, an old tree right by the spring, and you had to walk across that log." [60]

64

At the beginning of this century much of Main Street was still residential, but by the mid 1920s most buildings were in commercial use. The businesses at 203–207 Main Street, *left*, were typical of Annapolis enterprise. MdHR G 1936–1134A

"Here it seemed to me that the commercial life was dominated, or at least was well represented, by people who were, to me, cosmopolitan. I had a roommate who was from New York City. He said he felt very much at home in Annapolis. Here he had lived in Manhattan, but he said he felt very much at home in Annapolis because of the cosmopolitan nature of the town.

It was a vivid place and a place with a personality. Every store had its own personality. And the per-

sonality seemed to be wrapped up in the man who owned it, the owner and operator of that business. The proprietors were there running the place themselves and greeting you behind the door and serving you behind the counter. You knew who they were, whether they were Jew or gentile, you knew that they were the proprietor." [61]

"In those days the center was down there around the waterfront area. You had your A&P markets. And you had your vegetables there right at the market. And you had your seafood. You had your hardware stores, your marine supply stores, right there. You had your clothing stores, you had your—well, any-

Small family-owned grocery stores were everywhere, but by 1926, when Greenwald's Community Market was situated at 34 Market Space, the A&P chain—known locally as "the tea stores"—already had six locations in town. MdHR G 2140–194A

thing you'd find in a mall-type area. You had your shoe repair shops right there.

It was very convenient and you could walk to everything. You had your theaters within a couple of blocks. Anything that you could possibly want was in the downtown area of Annapolis. That was the town then. Anything that was needed to equip a house for living or survival you could find within a block or two of downtown Annapolis." [62]

The 1930 census listed twenty-eight automobile-related businesses in Annapolis. Andrew Krause Chevrolet, located at 900 West Street in 1926 when this photograph was made, was one of six car dealerships at the time. MdHR G 1804–266

"Cars were a long while catching on here in Annapolis. When they first started, you didn't go through any examining or anything. You bought a car, you got a license, and somebody told you what to do. My grandfather bought a car—the fact is, he bought three cars to start an agency here in town—and I think he got in the car, and he took his foot off the brake, and he ended up on John Dorr's corner. He never tried it again." [63]

Prohibition came early to Annapolis when, in 1918, the secretary of the navy declared that no liquor could be sold within five miles of any naval installation. By the time this group passed the jug in Bay Ridge c. 1925, many Annapolitans were making their own. MdHR G 2140–181

"People paid good service to Prohibition, but the fact of the matter is, they sort of drank as usual. My father and my grandfather never were excessive drinkers, but they had a five-gallon keg, which they kept down in the basement; and on fall or winter afternoons, they and some of their other gentlemen friends would go down there and eat oysters and have a little sip. And when the five-gallon keg would get empty, my father would put me in the rumble seat of his car and drive down to St. Mary's County. Down in St. Mary's County there was a gas station with two pumps. One pump pumped gasoline and the other pump pumped rye. That's the truth. So he would gas up his car and he would fill up his keg and saddle up and come on home again, and that would be it for the next few months. When it got empty, we'd go back and do it again.

I remember the day that they repealed the Volstead Act and people were running around shooting guns up in the air and banging on pots and pans and whooping and yelling, and that was the end of it. I was little, but I asked my parents what all the racket was.

My grandfather Worthington drank sparingly, but when he drank, he drank rye. And he drank it neat. I asked him once why he didn't mix it with water like the other people would. He said that he read the Bible, and he said that he decided that there were too many sinners drowned in the flood and he didn't want to use any of that water to dilute perfectly good whiskey. So he just drank a glass of it neat." [64]

Virtually everyone in town donned colonial costumes and participated in historical tableaux. Honored guests included President Calvin Coolidge and Governor Albert C. Ritchie, pictured here on the steps of the Chase-Lloyd House. MdHR G 2140–135A

1912.

Planners for Colonial Day, held on May 15, 1928, envisioned the event as the first of what they hoped would be an annual celebration of the city's colonial heritage. Dozens of school children danced around Maypoles in front of McDowell Hall, and hundreds of adults attended a ball that night in the State House. MdHR G 1754–19

"They had two Maypoles on St. John's campus. I was a boy in the larger group. My first cousin was a girl in the smaller group. We came down the hill holding hands, the boys and the girls, and we wove in and out, and it went over so big, we had to go back and do it again." [65]

"Colonial Day was in May 1928. Four or five kids, we decided that the garments the ladies were wearing, the hoop skirts, would make beautiful targets. So we paraded up to where we were in a very strategic position—that was in front of the State House—when the group passed. We thought we could have a lot of fun and practice our accuracy. We took rubber bands and we got little tiny staples, and we targeted the ladies in the hoop skirts. We'd plant these little staples in them and hear the sound of them popping. We had a great, great time doing that sort of thing. So I guess my impression of the parade and the event, and so forth, was that, gee, there were so many people and so many targets, wasn't it fun!

But it was a very festive and elegant affair. And, of course, there were so many historical structures, and it wasn't as crowded with automobiles, so that it made it seem almost as if it belonged in the colonial era. The cars that were around town were ordered not to park or be part of the festivities at all. I can't remember any cars moving at the time. It was all people in the carriages, walking and having a great time. The participants, as well as the viewers, were all celebrating." [66]

Edythe Campbell paused in front of the post office on Church Circle c. 1925 to have her picture taken. MdHR G 2140–279

"One of my memories, going back to my college days, was the girls coming down for dances. Very beautiful women, dressed to kill, would come off that train carrying their hatboxes and wearing spike heels. And looking very spiffy and being greeted by these handsome midshipmen, and walking, whole gangs of them, down to Carvel Hall or to the various drag houses around. It was either Carvel Hall or the drag houses, in those days.

I just remember thinking, at the time, that the most beautiful women in America—at least in the East—showed up in Annapolis on hop weekends. And women dressed differently then. These were all undergraduates. They were stylish, fashionable. They'd be wearing good-looking camel's hair coats, or some of the more affluent ones would have fur collars and things like that. I just remember the very good-looking women. Beautiful women and good-looking men. That was part of the ambience of Annapolis, these handsome young people." [68]

By 1929, when this patriotic group assembled on the steps of its Prince George Street entrance, Carvel Hall was the most popular hotel in Annapolis. MdHR G 1804–79

"Outside of the post office there used to be a big wide area for a flagpole. And we used to go down there to skate. Quite a few kids did. They'd meet there and skate in the afternoon. We sat on the steps and we'd chat. And then, going home, you'd probably go down Northwest Street. I knew girls on Northwest Street, they went to school. Minnie and Betsy. Yes, I stopped and chatted and talked with them. Then we would all go to Doc Thomas' and get a soda or something sweet." [67]

With two men's colleges in the city, Annapolis was a magnet for eligible and attractive young women. MdHR G 2140–419

In 1929, members of the religious community at St. Mary's Church chatted in the gardens adjacent to the former home of Charles Carroll of Carrollton.
MdHR G 2140–429

The Loyal Order of Moose met every Friday night at the Moose Home on West Street, c. 1930. MdHR G 1804–66

"When I was very young, six or seven years old, dogs literally slept down at the foot of Main Street. I went to St. Mary's grammar school and high school and Mother was a Catholic and Daddy was Episcopalian. And when you'd go over to the church, for Mass or stations of the cross, I remember there was that old brown mongrel, quite large, probably some Chesapeake Bay, who would wander through the open door and sleep on the cool marble in the middle of the aisle, and the priest would just step over him as he went around doing the stations of the cross. Nobody would pay much attention to the dog. He'd also come to Mass. He was probably very religious." [69]

"In my earliest recollection, the trash pickup was by Richard G. Chaney, who had the livery stable on the corner of Colonial Avenue and West Street and the storage on the corner of West Street and Southgate Avenue. One of the businesses went to one son and one went to the other when he died. He had a house there where part of the Annapolis Hotel is, which later was the Moose home, up on West Street, high above the street.

He had a little two-wheeled horse-drawn wagon with one man riding on it. A two-wheeled horse wagon, the trash was picked up by that. I think the hospital parking lot behind the hospital, bounded by the creek and Shaw Street and South Street there, I think that was land that was filled in by being the dump." [70]

"We lived on Fleet Street at the time, 1 Fleet Street. And there was a lady who lived up the street, a black woman, who ran the numbers. She would come down the street and she'd have her purse. And it seemed like it was always full of money, change. People would play pennies, nickels, dimes, quarters.

Well, one day, because of the summer heat, she collapsed right in front of the house. And my sister ran upstairs to get Mother. And she came down and there she was just passed out from the heat and age. She was old, too, so it was probably a combination of both. The heat just got to her.

So some other people were crowding around and Mother said, 'Pick her up and bring her in.' So they brought her into the house and Mother said, you know, 'Put her on the bed.' And we applied some cold towels to her face and hands, and she came around.

Well, later on that afternoon my sister and I were playing outside again. And I could hear some of the black ladies relating what had happened. And it was like nothing they'd ever seen before, that a white woman had picked up a black woman—up off the street—and put her in her own bed! It was a scene of wonder to them that something like that had happened." [71]

In downtown Annapolis, residential streets are always just around the corner from commercial areas. Cornhill and Fleet streets, *at right* c. 1930, empty into Market Space.
MdHR G 1672–3817L

"We had a great big hardware store, Henry B. Myers, which extended from West Street to Cathedral Street. And on the Cathedral side was a big tile block building of theirs where they kept all the hay and the seed and the feed and everything the farmers needed, and they came to town for this.

The building was divided off into three sections across the front of it. There was the households section—all the ladies would go there in those days if they needed something for the kitchen. In the middle was another section, and then there was a hardware side.

When we were little kids, the feed building and the hay building in back of Henry B. Myers on the Cathedral Street side caught fire. It

The Henry B. Myers Company was an institution at 45–49 West Street for more than sixty years. In addition to the hardware store, *left* c. 1930, Myers also operated a feed mill at West and Jefferson streets and a coal yard in the WB&A freight yard. MdHR G 1936–1590

was the worst sight I ever saw in my life. All the families and children were sent out of the neighborhood to Lafayette Avenue. And I could see enormous flames reaching into the sky. It was an awful fire, one of the biggest fires around here. They vacated everybody off the block."

[72]

Henry B. Myers was always well supplied with the latest in gadgets and conveniences, especially in the housewares department, *below*, c. 1935. MdHR G 1890–2979

Community Market, seen here at its new location at 32 Market Space c. 1935, was typical of the many small grocery stores in Annapolis. MdHR G 2140–235

"I started with A&P in 1937, when you waited on everybody behind the counter. A customer would come in and they'd say, 'I want a can of peas.' And you'd run down and get it and bring it up. We used to weigh all our own sugar, our own butter. If you wanted a piece of sharp cheese, I'd go back and cut it off the wheel and wrap it. We used to sell Snyder's potato chips, and they'd bring one of them three-pound cans and dump it in the big glass bin. And this is about all you'd sell the whole week.

In those days, it was all neighborhood stores. You used to fight to get somebody from Munroe Court to come down to 60 West Street. Plus, we used to deliver. The first job I had was delivering groceries. We had the big, old two-wheeled cart. And I can remember the Mustermans. John Musterman used to work for Strange & White. He lived in Munroe Court. Well, they used to come to our store once in a while. Freddy Tomanio, who ran 149 West Street, saw me taking groceries up there, and, of course, he raised hell for us taking his customers away.

Everything was wrapped in brown paper. If you bought your groceries from me, I'd get them all together, and I'd write it all down on the bag and add it up and ring it up on the old hand cash register. And then I'd have to get out my big brown paper and set everything on there and wrap it and then tie it up with old black creosote string. That's how we got it to you.

If you bought five pounds of sugar and two cans of peas and a can of corn and a loaf of bread, we'd put it all in one thing and just wrap it up. We didn't have those big bags in them days. Those big brown bags didn't show up until about 1939, when supermarkets opened up." [73]

"My grandmother immigrated to this country. Things were bad in the old country, and they thought she'd have a better chance of making something out of her life if she came to this country instead of staying in Germany where they were all so poor. She came to this country when she was fourteen years old and she couldn't speak a word of English. She had a tag on her coat and she was under the protection of the captain of the ship. She had relatives in Annapolis and she worked for them.

She got married, then she had a barroom saloon, and she had that for a number of years before Prohibition. It was at 236 West Street. After Prohibition came, my grandmother got rid of the saloon and she had a confectionery store, and then it was a restaurant. She had her home there, the store was in the front of the house. She had sundries and patent medicine and penny candy and ice cream and sundaes. Then later on she bought this machine that made sandwiches. Her crabcake sandwiches cost fifteen cents. Then she had another addition put on and she had a restaurant and she served meals. All they ever called it was Maggie Miller's.

She had five children and ran the business herself. She was a self-made woman." [74]

Maggie Miller's was located at 236 West Street in a building that no longer exists. The business began as a saloon, but changed with the times and became a confectionery during Prohibition. *At left,* Maggie Miller posed by the front door. MdHR G 2140–383

Maggie Miller's is remembered fondly by many Annapolitans as a favorite place to stop for ice cream after church on Sunday, and Maggie Miller's crabcake recipe is still famous. MdHR G 2140–384

Members of the Forest Hills Wesley Methodist Chapel congregation, including a few children, posed on the steps of the church that still stands at Forest Hills and Bay Ridge avenues in Eastport. This picture was made about the time of the chapel's rededication in 1930. MdHR G 2140–480

"A typical Sunday was to go to Sunday school in the morning and to stay for church at eleven o'clock, and many times to go back at night. Usually we spent quite a bit of time in church on Sunday. The church was a pivotal place in the black community not only for worship, but also for socializing. There were suppers and dinners and all kinds of activities were centered around the church." [75]

Stanton School still stands at 92 West Washington Street—it has been transformed into a community center. In 1930, students and faculty gathered for this group portrait. MdHR G 2140–277

"I graduated from high school in '54, so I would have left Stanton right around, oh, 1948, '47, somewhere in there. Let's see, it would have been '48 because I went to Bates in the seventh grade. Because we didn't have an integrated school, obviously. One of the biggest things I remember is, in thinking back then, that no one in our school dressed in distaste. Very rare was it that anyone wore dungarees or jeans to school. Everyone was extremely neat. And I remember that emphatically. No one hooked school. It was almost like a pressure from the city, from everyone, to go to school. And those few individuals who were truants and who didn't come to school or hooked school or smoked cigarettes, which was a very bad thing in those days, were looked down upon, considered really wild and woolly people." [76]

"We grew up on stories about oyster pirates on the Bay. And living right down on the creek and with the boatyards around, you could hang around the boatyards if you were quiet and listen to the old timers tell stories of the oyster pirates on the Bay. And, of course, oyster piracy was alive and well in those days, in fact, it was until the fifties.

The state of Maryland had rules concerning the harvesting of oysters. You essentially, in those days, had two ways of harvesting oysters. You'd dredge oysters with sailboats, with skipjacks, bugeyes, pungies or schooners. Nowadays, just the skipjacks are left, but there used to be hundreds and hundreds of craft out there. And certain areas of the Bay would be set aside for the dredge boats.

Then the tongers came along, and the tongers would have oyster tongs, the rakes on long wooden handles. And they would be restricted to the shallower waters that they could work without a big expensive boat, that they could reach with a hand-held rig. So they would have their areas, the tongers would have their areas and the dredge boats would have their areas, and you would be allowed so many bushels a day to keep them from wiping everything out. There was a very strong demand for oysters then as there is now.

Greed always rears its head, and back in the 1880s and 1890s, they would shanghai guys off the waterfront in Baltimore and in Annapolis. They would feed them knockout drops and they'd wake up on an oyster boat and they'd keep them on the boat and work them through the entire oyster season, and would not pay them. If they were lucky they would be put ashore alive. If they were unlucky, they would be paid off with the boom. That is, they would jibe the boat when they were not looking, and the boom would knock them overboard and they would drown and they would just be listed as a casualty. The dredge boats would invade the tongers' territory and vice versa. There was contention between Maryland and Virginia, and contending with everybody else was the Maryland oyster navy. They had several boats with cannon on them and they would have shoot-outs out on the Bay. Cannon would be blazing, cannon balls would be flying, rifles would be crackling." [77]

The Weems family lived at 9 Southgate Avenue, for some years the headquarters for the Weems System of Navigation. Music was so much a part of the Weems' social life that the children formed an orchestra called the Southgate Syncopaters: Bee Weems, saxophone, "Boo" Smith, guitar, Charles Fox, trumpet, Red Alexander, drum, and Missy Weems, piano. MdHR G 2140–388

"The Weems family had an impromptu orchestra that they called the 'Southgate Syncopaters, creators of novelty music. We always practice, we never play.' The Southgate Syncopaters was a rare outfit that was assembled by my brother-in-law. Philip would blow this bugle loudly from the third floor, and it would reverberate all around the creek. And then when the musicians heard that, they would all gather.

I had had a smattering of piano instruction when I was about six to twelve years old, and so I arrived there one day when the Southgate Syncopaters were trying to get organized, and I offered to play the piano. I then made a colossal blunder, though. I asked them what key they were playing in. I know that I was not asked to come back and play anymore." [78]

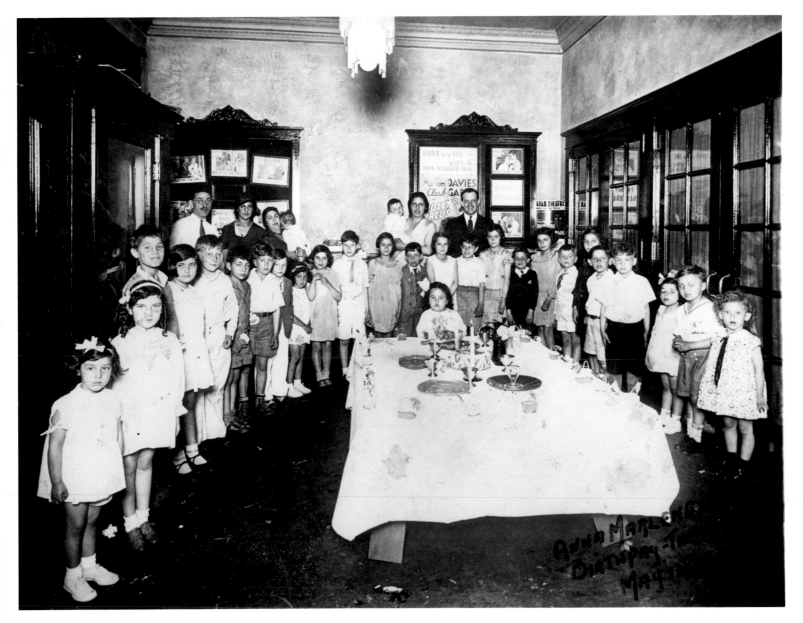

In 1926, the Star Theatre was purchased by Sam and Lena Eisenstein, who lived in an apartment upstairs for several years. Anna Eisenstein's third birthday party was held in the theater lobby on May 13, 1932. Some of the children in attendance were: Charlotte Gilden, Beverly Kramer, Lionel Brooks, Donald Levy, Stanley Berman, Edith Earle, Estelle Levy, Irene Richman, and Jackie Zelko. MdHR G 2140–411

"My father proposed to my mother in 1925, and they were married in February of 1926 in Baltimore. And when they were married, they immediately came to Annapolis. They came here to buy a butcher shop on the corner of Northwest and Calvert Street. And at the same time they came to buy the butcher shop, they looked across the street, and there was a For Sale sign on the theater. And my father turned to my mother and asked, 'Wouldn't you rather own a theater than a butcher shop?' And my mother said, 'Yes.'

On holidays, especially Christmastime, he had free movies on Saturday mornings for children, and the governor would come and speak to the children, and then there would be refreshments served. There was really an emotional effort put into making the business a community venture, something the community could take pride in." [79]

Members of the Booklovers' Club, pictured *at right* on April 11, 1931, were mostly residents of Murray Hill . MdHR G 2140–229A

"Everybody had a maid. The maid came at eight o'clock in the morning seven days a week. On Thursdays and Sundays, they left at two o'clock. On the other five days, they stayed until seven o'clock in the evening, after the evening meal, to wash the dishes. I think we paid them eight dollars a week.

The black community held funerals and excursions on Thursday afternoons, because that was their day off. Church suppers were always on Thursday evening, because the maids didn't work and so that was a good time to go to church suppers." [80]

FOLLOWING PAGES:

Eastport baseball team at the Annapolis ball park on West Street extended. MdHR G 2140–196

"Our social life was definitely the Jewish community. There were the German Jews, who came from better-educated families. They were the token Jews in the Elks, the token Jews in Kiwanis, Masons. They finally had Jews in the Masons. The Jews had to start their own Masonic lodge here, but there were these two or three Jews that belonged to the non-Jewish Masons. They were also successful professionals, or they were businessmen. And then there was my father, who was not a German Jew. World War II and Hitler made every Jew realize that there was no demarcation according to country of origin." [81]

The Kiwanis Club included many prominent members of the Annapolis business community in its membership when the group gathered at the foot of Main Street at Christmastime in 1933. The brick building on the left was part of the Amoco gasoline station once located in the circle at Market Space. MdHR G 2140–301

"Old Dr. Anderson used to take me every Sunday during baseball season out to the Annapolis ball park, and that's where now you have Erol's and Acura and Phipps Buick, out in that area.

That was the old Annapolis ball park, and it was fantastic. At least I thought it was the greatest thing in the world. Had the old wooden bleachers with a roof over them. It angled down the third base line, and then squared off behind home plate, and then angled down to the first base line—it had a big wooden fence all the way around it.

And 'Snake' Baker was the concessionaire—concessionaire supreme. He used to sell everything from Coke to Cracker Jacks. It was just amazing. Snake was a hundred years old then, from what I remember. He was the oldest-looking man I ever saw in my life. He used to carry around those heavy things of Coke and all, and he would yell and scream, you know, out there, what he was selling. Somebody up in the stands would yell, 'Hey, Snake. Send me up a bag of peanuts.' And he would yell back, 'Let me see your money first.' You know, things like this.

Everybody knew everybody that was there. You went into a ball park and there were a couple hundred there, you knew 199 of them. And I remember one player in particular. This is another guy that was probably one of my heroes. His name was Bill Jewett, and he played center field. And he used to have this thing where—and nobody ever caught onto this—but say a guy was on first base, okay? A guy would hit the ball, a ground ball, say, over second and out to center, and Bill Jewett would come charging in for that ball. And he would field it cleanly, but he would turn like he missed it, and he would pretend like he was chasing it. And the guy who hit the ball would round first base and he would start to second. Well, Bill would stop all of a sudden and throw the ball in to the second baseman, and they had the guy out by twenty feet. And they never caught on to this! These dumb teams would come into Annapolis, and Bill Jewett would pull this on them all the time.

And I remember 'Feet' Myers. That's another name, 'Feet' Myers, because his feet were so big. He played third base. And I remember Wyatt. I forget his first name, but Wyatt was a pitcher and I believe he was a southpaw. He was a big, burly guy. Oh, gosh, these guys were fantastic." [82]

The Bounelis family owned the Capitol Restaurant and Hotel at 200 Main Street. During the 1930s and 1940s, many of Annapolis' eating establishments were operated by families of Greek descent, often by first generation immigrants. MdHR G 1672–3817O

"I remember the Capitol Restaurant and Hotel. My grandmother went in there. There were people in there, Bounelis, that worked in there or owned it, I never knew which, that she had to stop and visit. It was where Hampton House is on Main Street now. At that time it was one of the better restaurants in Annapolis. A lot of the midshipmen and their families when they were here in town would eat there. It had a small hotel over top that you'd enter mainly through State Circle." [83]

Trautwein's hardware store at 136 Dock Street sold everything from groceries to gasoline. In 1935, *above*, the staff at Trautwein's included Donald Covington, Martha Sullivan, Jack Flood, Gene Butler, and Walter "Rabbit" Little. MdHR G 2140–200

"'Rabbit' Little drove a mule for my grandfather, Joe Trautwein. I used to get a big kick out of riding over to Eastport. It was just like going to Europe, riding with Rabbit. When we would go across the bridge, as he would go past the drawbridge, he would make a noise that sounded like a horn.

My grandfather was friends with everybody in the police department. And this one day, they called up my grandfather and said, 'Mr. Trautwein, we got Rabbit locked up. We got him up here for impersonating an automobile.'" [84]

"I can remember now, us thinking—we'd be talking like a big thing was going to happen. We were going to go over town to the old Republic Theatre to the movies. And, of course, if you went to the movie—and usually it would be a western on Friday with a serial behind it or a good movie—you always stayed to see two or three shows.

Plus I always remember it as being air-conditioned. And so on a real hot summer day it felt very good to get in that air-conditioning. And we would stay—like if we went over at six o'clock—we'd stay till the movie closed that night and then come home. It was a big expedition to go over to that big city of Annapolis and see all the excitement and everything.

We never wore shoes in the summertime. I never put a pair of shoes on from the day school was out until the day I went back to school. We'd even walk over to Annapolis and go the movie barefooted. You know, it was just a tradition. An Eastport boy went barefoot." [85]

The Republic Theatre, 187 Main Street, was a magnet every Saturday for the children of Annapolis who went each week to see the latest cowboy movies and to find out what happened next in the serial. In the early 1950s, the Republic, seen *below* in 1936, became the Playhouse Theatre. MdHR G 1672–3817Q

Now restored to its colonial appearance and called Middleton's Tavern, 2 Market Space was known for many years as Mandris' Confectionery. MdHR G 1672–3817N

"I was born in Greece. I came to Annapolis in 1938. When I moved to Annapolis, I went to work down in Mandris' Restaurant. My wife's father had the place and he told me, 'If you come into Annapolis, I'm going to retire whether you take the place over or not.'

One day, three fellows come in here and say to me, 'How would you like to feed twenty-five people a day? We are going to be here tomorrow morning at eight o'clock.'

In the morning, before I know it, the place filled up. This boy Wilson comes in and he says, 'What the heck is wrong? Where is the people that's going to serve us and all?'

I says, 'Look, you young fellow, you're a good man. Be a Greek for one day, here's an apron. We'll serve the people. We've got to do something.' And they stayed with me for better than a month and a half. After people seen that I was busy all the time, then I got more busy—I couldn't handle it.

When I started the place I used to be open from six o'clock in the morning to twelve o'clock at night. That lasted for three years. I didn't know Annapolis had a West Street.

The main thing is to have good food. When someone wasn't satisfied twice, I used to tell them, 'Mister, I have tried my hardest to please you, and I cannot please you.' I take a box of cigars and I says, 'Here, take what you want and smoke it and go and try someplace else. If you like it, stay there. If you don't, come back, but don't complain.'" [86]

Neighborhood stores, like Rebecca Levy's at 206 West Street, kept many families afloat during the Depression because they allowed customers to buy on credit. MdHR G 2140–354

"My mother had a grocery store at West Street and Madison Place. My father died when I was six, and so my mother had this grocery store. She provided for us, made our living there. She didn't have a choice. Either that, or I don't know what would have happened to us.

My mother didn't only sell groceries, she sold linens, bed linens, sheets and blankets, and it was like a general store. It also was a place for people to come. I think they came and made that their social life. There were some women who came and stayed there practically all day, or at least half a day, until it was time to go home and fix their dinner. It was a gathering place for people in the neighborhood.

My mother was a very outgoing woman who sort of gathered people around her. She also could tell you how to run your life, and I guess she befriended everybody. I suppose that was a good part of it.

My mother used to go to Baltimore at four o'clock in the morning to a wholesale place. It was on Camden Street in Baltimore. That's another reason she did well. She bought her own fresh produce, and she would go at four o'clock in the morning in that little old car—and the way she drove!—and bring it back." [87]

Franchised fast food came to Annapolis in the form of the Little Tavern, of which there were two. The first was at 84 West Street, seen *above* in 1937; later, another opened on Main Street. MdHR G 2140–325

"There was the Little Tavern and the death-burgers. Didn't we call them death-burgers? They were full of onions, and after you ate them, you had a funny feeling in your stomach about ten minutes later. But they were ten cents and they were packed with onions on a roll. They were so cheap, I guess, that we loved to go in and do that. And we also went to Bernstein's. My best friend and I would go to Bernstein's and eat potato chips and chocolate Cokes. If that isn't decadent, I don't know what is." [88]

"We used to go all the way to the top of the State House dome. That was one place we would go on Sundays because we could go up and see all of Annapolis." [89]

"This is the Board of Directors for the Company for the Restoration of Colonial Annapolis. That's Admiral David F. Sellers. He was superintendent of the Naval Academy at the time. And that fat guy is Harry W. Nice, he was governor. And that's Mrs. D. Mershon Garrison, a woman of some importance around here—and she thought so, too.

Now this fellow came up from Virginia—Dr. Goodwin from Williamsburg. He came up to tell us all about Williamsburg. Just behind the admiral, that's Dr. James Magruder. He was assistant rector at St. Anne's at the time. This was Arthur Trader, and he was the head of the Land Office. This is George Forbes, he was a lawyer in Baltimore. And there's old Amos W. W. Woodcock. At one time he was United States attorney and former president of St. John's. That's young Louis Phipps, a mayor of Annapolis, and Paul Kieffer, he was on the faculty at St. John's. I'm next to him. And that's Mrs. John M. Green in the hat. She married late in life; she was Sara Sutherland.

Back here is Peter Magruder. He was for years secretary of the Naval Academy, and when he retired, they abolished the job. He was also commodore of the Annapolis Yacht Club. This one is Marion Lazenby, who was head of the Annapolis Dairy. This is

The Company for the Restoration of Colonial Annapolis posed on the steps of the superintendent's quarters at the Naval Academy in 1937. MdHR G 2140–134A

Wilson Evitt, general manager of the dairy and Annapolis Utilities. Wilson was a very nice guy. During the war he was a pilot, he was in Rickenbacker's squadron. The day the war ended he flew a mission, and when he came back he got out of the plane, and from that day forward he never got into another airplane, commercial or otherwise. He figured his luck ran out.

Behind Peter Magruder is Howard Atterberry, he came from up in New England somewhere and came down here to retire. Next to him is Ridgely Melvin, who was a lawyer here in town. Next to him is Albert H. McCarthy, who at that time owned Carvel Hall. Dave

Jenkins was editor of the *Evening Capital*. Next to him is Mayor Will McCready. And this head, way up in the corner is an unidentified man from Williamsburg.

The company was the bright idea of a few people. I drew up its first charter when it was incorporated. And we used to meet and meet and meet and talk and talk and talk. And then the war came along and nobody ever heard another thing about it." [90]

The colonial Governor's Mansion was located on the present grounds of the Naval Academy. When the academy bought the building in 1866, a new mansion, *above,* was built on State Circle. In 1936, Governor Harry W. Nice decided to alter the original Victorian architecture to a Georgian style that he thought more in keeping with Annapolis' colonial heritage.
MdHR G 1804–510

"One day I was at the Governor's Mansion and Mrs. O'Conor came in in this beautiful white and silver dress. It was a black-tie affair, their silver anniversary. I had been up there just about all day. And she said, 'Do you want to go downstairs and see my gifts in the playroom?' I saw silver that I know I'd never seen before in my life. They had silver on the pool table, on the Ping-Pong table, and all along the side walls.

So after my visit in there I walked over there where they were dancing, and other people came around. Was I a guest? Was I having a good time? Could I dance? You would have thought I was a guest. Here's this big ball, and here's this little black kid coming by in a skirt and sweater and plaits. I'm sure I wore braids back in those days.

I went home that night with cartons of Coke, bottles of champagne. The chauffeur brought me home. They had bagged me chicken croquettes, cake, and this fancy ice cream that looked like a picture, but it was ice cream. By the time I got home, it had melted. But I didn't care. I was so happy. I think if I could have saved everything to this day, I would have. It was the prettiest thing that I had ever witnessed." [91]

City Dock, seen *at right* from the air c. 1935–1937, reveals the ever-changing cityscape. The gas station at Market Space was torn down in the late 1960s. MdHR G 2258–13

"I read the local paper. I knew what was going on, and I saw the signs of segregation. There were four restrooms down at the gas station on the City Dock, the Amoco station. And this struck me then as sort of emblematic of the absurdity of it all. There was a building there, next to the gas station, also done up in Georgian style. And there was a men's room and a women's room, except there were two men's rooms and two women's rooms. So everything had to be doubled because of this. That was the most blatant sign of it." [92]

"Then, of course, the big attraction in Annapolis at that time—and, of course, to this day, really—was the Naval Academy. That was just such a big thing in our life. We got into things at the academy through my brother-in-law. Our life became very exciting when it was very involved with the academy.

In the summertime, a typical day would be getting up in the morning, and then getting our work done—Mother would give us our work to do—getting our work done fast, because we had such an incentive to get through the work to get out and play. And then we'd go over to the academy.

We would play three sets of tennis in the morning. We had a whole bunch of kids who lived in the academy, and kids who lived on Duke of Gloucester Street. Then we would end up at the indoor navy pool.

And then, in the winter, plebe basketball would start about one o'clock and we'd go to that game, and that would finish at about 2:30. Then we would go to the varsity basketball game. When the basketball would end, we'd go over to Macdonough Hall, and water polo and swimming would be being held then, and wrestling. We would go and stand in line. The admiral and his wife would be in line first to congratulate them or commiserate with them if they lost. And all the O'Neills would line up right behind, all of us, congratulating, 'Just dandy.' Shaking hands, telling them how wonderful they were, or how sad we felt for them." [93]

View across Dewey Basin to Macdonough and Luce halls, where many athletic events took place, 1937. MdHR G 2258–17

On November 21, 1937, a dramatic fire at Carvel Hall, *left*, forced the hotel to close for several months. MdHR G 1943–26

"The first Carvel Hall fire was on a Sunday morning. As I came out of Sunday school, I saw this huge black cloud of smoke going up over the town. So I ran home for permission to go to the fire, but my parents said that we were going to church and maybe we'd take me down there after church. And so I stood there on the sidewalk watching these great billows of ever-changing colors of smoke as the water would hit it, and all of my buddies, 'Come on Tom, let's go.'

So I didn't get down there until after church and, of course, they had brought fire equipment down from Glen Burnie and Baltimore and over on the ferryboat from the Eastern Shore, any way to try to put this thing out. It was just a terrible fire and it just about destroyed the new portion of Carvel Hall. Fortunately not the old portion, but tremendous damage was done. It was a huge fire, by far the biggest one that I ever saw." [94]

"I remember a lot of horses and wagons and buggies, for several reasons. Number one, there was still quite a few left and, number two, my strongest memories are of the thirties—and the thirties are the Depression years and some people who had motor vehicles couldn't afford to run them, so they dusted the old buggy off and hooked up the horse and came to town." [95]

Ice wagons, like this one on Pinkney Street c. 1939, were a familiar sight for many years. Shiplap House can be seen on the right. MdHR G 908–39

West Annapolis is a misnomer because the community is actually located on the northern bounds of the city. The area began to develop after the turn of the century when Annapolitans sought homes outside the traditional city limits. This aerial view was made in October 1939 from above College Creek. The B&A Short Line Railroad tracks appear in the foreground. Today, Rowe Boulevard follows almost the same route across the creek. MdHR G 2140–124

"We played over here in West Annapolis, which is now part of the Naval Academy where the Quonset huts are. That used to be a big field. We played football there, and that field was also used for the annual West Annapolis carnival.

There was a big florist right near Graul's. The whole area was quite undeveloped, of course. There wasn't any Rowe Boulevard or bridge. And the only thing that came over in this area was the WB&A electric trains. So the whole area was undeveloped other than one or two places. There was even a little West Annapolis train station.

In those days you did a lot of walking. You didn't have the transportation, you didn't have buses or anything like that. You could get to it by coming up King George Street. That was the only bridge across College Creek." [96]

In 1868, the Naval Academy purchased land across College Creek fronting on the Severn River. A naval hospital was built on the property, and various athletic facilities, including a baseball stadium and a golf course, were located there when this aerial was made. Seaplanes, used for aviation training in the 1940s and 1950s, are pictured *above*. MdHR G 2140–226

"During the Second World War my mother belonged to the Red Cross, and the Red Cross ladies ran a cafeteria in the golf course building—the Naval Academy Golf Course which was where the swimming pool and the townhouses are now.

It was used during the war by the Red Cross to serve meals to service personnel attached to the academy. My mother would take me there sometimes with her to work. I was kept back in the kitchen or allowed to run around outside while they were serving. Sometimes other women brought their children and we would be allowed to go out on the golf course and run. I don't remember it being a real golf course with greens. I didn't know what they were at the time. They were just places where there was sand that was fun to jump in. I didn't ever see anybody playing on it, but I remember that it was beautiful and green." [97]

Although much altered since this photograph was made in 1939, these adjoining homes still stand at 56–62 Spa Road. MdHR G 2140–107

"My grandmother's sister lived at 55 Spa Road. And she had children, and next to her were some cousins. They were relatives, we were allowed to come up and play with them. And when we'd go uptown, like for a matinee, we associated with their school friends. But generally the downtown children stayed downtown, the children uptown stayed uptown in my day.

There were quite a few children who lived across the street on Spa Road. And they always came over into our back yard, and we enjoyed just being around in the house with the family. There was always something good to eat, always a pie, always a cake, always ice cream, always chicken. And we just enjoyed being around in the house. Of course, a lot of times we would get run out, because you know how some children just want to stay underneath the older folks. We'd get chased out sometimes so the older folks could enjoy themselves sitting and talking. And my family—I'm not bragging, but I'm telling you the truth—were more or less religious people, and so there wasn't a lot of drinking or any such thing." [98]

In 1938, a survey by the Annapolis Housing Authority showed that 38.4 percent of the available shelter in the city was sub-standard. The majority of families living in sub-standard housing were black. Like this instance in Calvert Court off Calvert Street in 1939, twenty-seven percent of Annapolis houses lacked flush toilets.
MdHR G 2140–106A

"My mom did domestic work. The family that she worked for offered to let the kids take a nice cold shower to cool off. In those days you were lucky if you had a bathroom in your house! Some houses did, and we did on College Avenue. It's the funniest thing. My grandmother's house was next door. She had an outhouse. She lived at 20 College Avenue, and we lived at 18, so we had a bathroom. The only thing, we didn't have any heat up there in the wintertime. But in the summer, it was great, a nice back window right over the tub. You could open up the window. We could get out on our back roof. It had one of those old tin roofs. When it rained, we could just go to sleep by hearing the noise." [99]

The old Eastport bridge connected Duke of Gloucester Street on the Annapolis side and Fourth Street in Eastport. Many Eastporters considered the journey across the bridge a trip to the big city. This 1939 aerial view shows how much smaller the Naval Academy was before it dredged the Severn River and Spa Creek in 1960 to create new athletic fields. MdHR G 2140–227

"I lived on the Eastport bridge. My grandfather was the bridge attendant there for twenty-seven years. We used to get out there with a pipe and stick it in the thing and turn it. We opened the bridge sixty-five times in an eighteen-hour period one time.

You had to be careful there if you were drinking any coffee. If a horse came on the bridge, even at a trot, the coffee would splash back and forth. If you left the coffee while the horse was running, then the coffee cup was empty when you got ready to drink it. Everything sloshed out of it.

One time I was there by myself, and someone wanted to get out about four o'clock in the morning and I didn't hear him. He tooted the horn and I didn't wake up. So pretty soon I heard this noise. And what he did was come up under the bridge and take the oars and beat on the bottom of the house, you know. That woke me up, and I opened the bridge.

My grandfather worked twenty-four hours a day, and I helped him when I could when I was there, when I wasn't in school. He lived his work. He enjoyed it. That was his life, him and that bridge." [100]

Eastport, seen here from the air c. 1939, was almost a self-sufficient village apart from Annapolis with many neighborhood businesses that supplied basic necessities. Eastporters depended on the maritime industry—they worked oyster beds, fished the abundant waters of the Chesapeake Bay, or built boats at the boatyards that lined the peninsula's perimeter. MdHR G 2140–228

"I'm actually the fifth generation—my children were the sixth generation—raised on the Eastport peninsula. And it comes from my mother's side of the family. My father came here in the navy, in the middle twenties. Met my mother, who was an Eastport girl. Married, and of course that's where I was born and raised. It was actually not Annapolis in those days, though. It was still part of Anne Arundel County. Yet, it was always considered Annapolis. And I think in 1950 we were annexed into the city.

Old Eastporters still resent that, too. We loved our identity as Eastporters and we like to be referred to as Eastporters, not Annapolitans, which we actually are.

I had an extremely good family life and an extended family, grandmother, great-uncles, father and mother. And growing up in Eastport was like paradise. I look at it now and I just wish that it would be more like it used to be so my children and grandchildren could enjoy it the way I did." [101]

McNasby Oyster Company started business on Compromise Street in Annapolis about 1906. By 1918, McNasby's had moved its operations to Second Street in Eastport, seen *at left* and *below* c. 1935. MdHR G 2140–43A

In the early 1900s, packing houses lined the Annapolis harbor area. In 1918, McNasby's employed thirty-two shuckers and paid them an average of twenty-eight dollars per week. MdHR G 2140–41A

"McNasby's designed the front entrance of the Eastport plant so you could get the product from the watermen with the booms and the lines and all the baskets to hoist the seafood up out of the vessels. And they were either dumped into a conveyor or wheel barrow or something and moved into the area for them to be selected—the oysters could be selected for different purposes, some for shucking, some to be sold on the half-shell, and some to be shipped as is.

You didn't have to have white gloves on and a mask and stuff like that. It was just individuals handling the product as it came through their station. The shuckers were mostly blacks. And there were whites, of course, too. It wasn't any question of segregation or anything. But it seemed like the blacks were the better workers, I guess, or at least they would work maybe for less. I don't know. It seemed to be that you saw more blacks than you did the whites at these places.

A lot of the shuckers lived right down in the dock area. Most of them lived along Fleet Street and Pinkney and parts of East Street. Also parts of Cornhill Street. That was your lower section, and down, of course, in the Randall Street area, you had blacks there. But they were mostly your water-oriented people, that lived down close, within walking distance of their occupation."

[102]

Attendance at church on Sunday was mandatory for all midshipmen until the early 1970s. Some attended services at the academy chapel, others formed church parties and marched into town to various churches and the local synagogue. Here, St. Mary's Church was filled with worshipers in uniform, c. 1940. MdHR G 1672–20,224D

"I remember the Governor Herbert O'Conor family. They went to St. Mary's and they would go to ten o'clock Mass Sundays. Mrs. O'Conor was a lovely, attractive woman and he was a handsome man. Of course, you're very impressed, the governor coming and sitting two or three seats in front of you.

There was a priest from St. Mary's who was assigned to the midshipmen then. They came to St. Mary's. Three battalions of Catholic midshipmen would come to seven o'clock Mass and one would come to ten o'clock. So we loved to go to ten o'clock, to see the O'Conors and to see the midshipmen." [103]

The bond between Annapolis and the Naval Academy was reinforced often through marriage. *At right*, the wedding party of Marge and Frederick Dowsett posed on June 4, 1938. MdHR G 2140–263

"I was a Depression bride. We just didn't have any money. If it hadn't been for friends bringing flowers and hams and sandwiches, I don't know what we would have done. We invited fifty people to the reception and a hundred people came. You couldn't get in the door. When I went to cut the cake in the middle of the living room, everybody was crowding in and I felt like: If they don't get out of the way I'm going to knife them with the sword. Finally, I said 'Some of you get out of here, I've got to cut the cake!'" [104]

Right, a company of midshipmen paused in front of 22–28 West Street on their way to the WB&A station, c.1940. MdHR G 2140–300

"They would take the entire midshipmen body to the Army–Navy game. They rented special trains from the Pennsylvania and the B&O and they loaded along the West Street station.

They would bring in one train for the team, and civilians and other people who wanted to go to the game would go on that team train. Then the day of the game, they brought in trains to take the regiment. Usually two, one from Pennsylvania and one from B&O. That was a big thing in my earliest years. My father would take me over to see the steam engine on the train.

The midshipmen would march through the city streets with a band, no matter what time they left. Sometimes they'd leave at four o'clock in the morning, and they'd march through the streets with a band.

When they came back, the band would play, and they would parade. In those days, they all wore leather heels and they marched much better then. If they won, they would chant the score, and you would go out and watch them come back in and whoop it up marching in ranks. I even knew St. John's students who would walk along the side of them. That was a real free-for-all and a party for which large crowds would turn out at midnight to see them come in on times when navy had won." [105]

The area between Prince George and King George streets, known as Hell Point, was appropriated by the Naval Academy in 1941. The property included a mixture of private homes, the steamboat and ferry wharves, packing houses, and the Johnson Lumber Company. This aerial, made October 10, 1939, shows what was lost when the properties were demolished. MdHR G 2140–115

"The Naval Academy had grabbed a chunk of Annapolis from time to time and in 1941 they were about to do it again. They wanted even more than they got, but they settled for what they took. They sent a gentleman down from Chicago who was sort of the chief appraiser for their Federal Land Bank. My father had a real estate and insurance business, and my father really hated to see this happen because he loved the old town, too.

They had the right to take it. In eminent domain, you could condemn private property for public use if you were an arm of the government and, indeed, they were. So my father figured that they couldn't be stopped, but if they had somebody working on the appraisal and perhaps being able to modify it constructively, at least it would ensure that the people would get more for their property than perhaps they would get if they did not have local knowledge working on it.

If you could say any area was economically depressed, it was Hell Point. It probably was anyway, but the crash coming in '29 and the Depression just made it tougher. I don't think anybody in Annapolis wanted to see the Naval Academy gobble up another chunk of the town. But I don't think the rest of Annapolis was as emotionally involved as was the immediate area down there." [106]

117

Hell Point embraced a wide mixture of social classes. Structures that were leveled on Holland Street, *below* in 1941, ranged from comfortable middle class homes to tenements. MdHR G 2140–205

Block Court was one of several narrow alleys in Hell Point. It ran parallel to Randall Street and dead-ended into King George Street and the Naval Academy. MdHR G 2140–208

"Holland Street is no longer in existence. The navy took it in. Holland Street was really Hell Point. That's where Hell Point was. There were some alleys in here where people lived—I won't say they lived—they existed there. That's all I can say. They were slums.

They had no indoor plumbing of any kind. Mr. Smiley used to go to see people on Holland Street and Mother used to send things to people on Holland Street. We usually had dinner in the middle of the day, and whenever there was any soup left over or stew or whatever, Mr. Smiley would take it to this one elderly woman he knew. She didn't have anything at all, and he would go down there and take things to her or to whoever else needed it. A couple of times he took me with him, but he wouldn't let me go in the houses. So I never really saw the interior of the houses, but I know that some of it was pretty bad. But

some of it was pretty good. Some of the houses were well kept. And if they owned their own house they kept it much better. But then the landlords—we had slum landlords then just like we do today." [107]

"In 1941, on Holland Street, the wreckers were tearing it down and we would go over there and help ourselves to the wreckage for firewood. Well, it seems that that was all government property. We were picked up by the security guards for stealing government property. They were going to put us in the jail for that. I can recall that some guy had me by the arm. He was very tight about it. And another workman there said, 'Oh, for Christ's sake, they're just kids coming over to get firewood. What are you going to lock them up for?' He did let us go eventually, but we were quite frightened about that." [108]

118

The navy bought the original site of Johnson Lumber Company along with the rest of the property at Hell Point in 1941. The location was ideal when most lumber arrived by boat. MdHR G 2140–212

"Johnson Lumber Company was at the foot of King George Street, next to the ferry. And that took up maybe half of the block behind Holland Street. And the other half was taken up with piers. There was a crab house down there, operated by the Grey family. There were some black families that lived back there." [109]

"There was hardly anything out this way on West Street, very little of anything. And then, as you went in town, it was all the black folks lived right on the road. And West Street, if you had a big rain, it flooded in there it was so low. They were all houses in there until you got down to Johnson Lumber Company. After Johnson's closed up down on King George Street, they moved out there.

And going in town, there was some old buildings there, old furniture stores there one time, long about where Tate Dodge is, and the Rainbow Cleaners was there when we still had the ball field where Phipps Buick is.

There was no Chinquapin Round

By 1945, *above*, Johnson's had settled in at 1901 West Street, where the property surrounding it was still largely farmland or woods. MdHR G 2140–262

Road. That was a horse track that used to go down to Vineyard Road, which belonged to old man Dickerhoff. He used to raise grapes and make wine down there. There was no Forest Drive. That was all farms down in there. Over where Lincoln Park is there, the commercial place, that was all a farm there. There was one old barn back in there. When we were kids, we used to go down there and help feed the horses." [110]

Like most of the city's historic homes, Ogle Hall remained a private residence well into the twentieth century. Its kitchen, seen *at left* c. 1940, was equipped with the modern conveniences of the day. During the 1940s, the house was purchased and renovated by the Naval Academy Alumni Association for its headquarters. MdHR G 1672–20,204X

"I remember the rationing during the war very well because you had to get gas rations. You had ration books for the grocery store. You didn't have sugar. My mother made her own butter. One of my earliest memories of my mother was of her walking around the house in the summertime with a pint jar of cream that she had taken off the top of the milk jugs. The milk was separated, and you could put a spoon, a specially-shaped sort of S-shaped spoon, down to cover the tiny neck of the milk part and pour off the cream. And mother would, over a period of several days, pour off the cream and save it, and then she would put it in this pint jar. And she would walk around the house with the pint jar in her hand, shaking it. And she would have butter, and she would turn it out on a dish, and then she would mark it. Sometimes, if I was very good, I could help.

Mother said that, on bread, she did not want margarine. It was my job to take the bag of margarine from the A&P that had the yellow dot of dye in the corner and squeeze it and mix the yellow dye into the white margarine. If you did a good job, it came out sort of this icky yellow color and it was fairly even, and that was what you used for most things that you used margarine for. It was soft, and it came in a plastic bag sealed at both ends, with this dye thing in one corner." [111]

123

By 1931, the county's black population had outgrown Stanton School, and Wiley Bates High School opened on Smithville Street. *Above*, a class poses on the steps, December 8, 1941. MdHR G 2140–233

"I remember when I was going to Bates High School, an all-black school, being invited over to Annapolis Senior High because we had a dynamite choir and a dynamite band. And I remember with all of the pride that it almost brings tears to my eyes, marching from Bates High School which was only two blocks away.

And we had a spiffy band, I mean, we were sharp. They say that all blacks have rhythm, I guess that maybe we do. By having that so-called natural rhythm, we were extra good. And we sang, too.

So we took the band and the choir over to Annapolis High. I remember seeing those white kids hanging out of the windows when we got there. And with such pride and, somewhat, humility, we walked in and they applauded. We cadenced over there and we had yellow Eisenhower jackets with these purple hats, and these purple pants with yellow stripes on them. And we wore what they call white buckskin shoes, and we were sharp. The choir came over en masse walking behind us.

We went into the auditorium. I don't know why we went over there, but it must have been an exchange of culture or something. Because, once again, there was prejudice here, but we tolerated each other to such a point that we could talk. I had white friends. I wouldn't go in their house and sit down and eat, but—that day, I remember going home—I've always been a very emotional man, and I remember going home and feeling filled up emotionally about having done that because we were black and these white kids, I guess they never realized that we were that talented. And we put on a show. I mean, they applauded." [112]

When it opened, Bates High School was out-fitted with top grade equipment like that shown in this science lab, c. 1945.
MdHR G 2140–232

"I don't recall when the bus transportation started, not for black people. They had bus transportation for whites many years before they had it for blacks. Anybody who came to high school, they would have to get out on Ritchie Highway and hitch-hike, hitchhike a ride down the road.

The first transportation for black children from South County, our PTA started that. We hired a man with a bus who went around in South County and picked up children and brought them to Stanton. That was interesting because those people, those black people, had nothing to pay that man with, and they used to give him eggs, chickens, turkeys, potatoes, anything, to help to pay for the children to get here. Rough goings.

Bates was overcrowded. I think Bates was built for 1,300, and after so many years, it had more than 1,700 in there. And when the Board decided to give some relief for it, they had more than 2,200 students. By that time there was bus transportation, and these were students who were coming from the borders of Baltimore and Calvert County, all over Anne Arundel County, because that was the only black high school.

They would have to catch a bus around seven-something, I guess, to get here. And they would go to sleep in class. The first thing, they didn't have anything to eat before they left home, and that long drive would almost set you crazy. When it got up around 2,200 people, that's when the Board of Education decided to open what they called the 'junior high school.' What they did was move the seventh grade out of the old Bates and put them in the old abandoned Stanton building on Washington Street." [113]

125

Regardless of race, religion was an important focus for many Annapolitans. *At left*, members of the congregation gathered at the First Baptist Church at 39 West Washington Street in 1943. MdHR G 2140–283

"We were a closely knit neighborhood with the center of life being the church. My parents were very religious and felt that our religious growth could best be nurtured in the church, so therefore whenever the church doors opened, we were there. All day Sunday and sometimes during the week. On Monday evening there was a Bible studies class at which attendance was mandatory in our family." [114]

"When I came home, I came in on a train from California to Baltimore. And my ticket was from San Francisco to Annapolis. So I had a ticket for the old B&A. This is before the B&A stopped running. And when I hit Camden Station, I was going down to get on the train, and old man Wilmer Shue was a motorman, and I said to him, 'Mr. Shue.' Because I knew him. I said, 'I just come halfway around the world.' Which I did—the Philippines here it was fourteen thousand miles.

I said, 'I hope this old trolley will give me a safe trip home.'

He said, 'Don't worry about it, boy.'

So when I got on the train, I sat right behind him. He had that little caboose up in front, you know, where he sat. We got to Wolf Street, two blocks away, and he run into an automobile. So he let the conductor off, and the conductor had to write it up. So we come on into Annapolis into Bladen Street.

And I went from the train station all the way to Madison Street, and I

During World War II, Annapolis had several clubs providing support to armed forces personnel. The armed services YMCA on Northwest Street, *above* c. 1943, offered gift-wrapping services during the holidays. MdHR G 2140–289

didn't have anybody says, 'Hi, Dean! Glad to see you home!' or anything. There was no parades or nothing. These guys from Vietnam, that's all they hollering about, 'They didn't have a parade for me when I got home.' I can't understand them. We all fought for freedom. That's what we were fighting for, including Vietnam. But there was no big to-do about it. So, I think I took a week off, and the following week I went back to my old job at A&P." [115]

Sparrow's Beach was located on the Chesapeake Bay southeast of Annapolis. *Above,* Mary Baden and Bea Coates visit with friends from Wilmington, Delaware, c. 1942. MdHR G 2140–447

"My father worked at the academy laundry for forty-some years. They used to have an annual picnic for all the employees of the academy at' Sparrow's Beach. We would go and catch these big duty boats that holds all these people, and they would take us down from there, around the Bay to go to the beach.

I almost drowned because my mother had brought me a bucket and shovel. Well, nobody ever said how to swim, and I just kept going out. And eventually the waves—I was real young, maybe six, maybe seven, I'm guessing—and I was walking, and the waves sort of took me under. And I knew it was just taking me out. And then I was like going to go to sleep, and all of a sudden I was yanked. My neighbor just saw a bottom of a foot way out in the water. She said, 'That looks like a child's foot.' And she yanked, and 'It's Peggy!' Of all people, me.

Old Dr. Greene, one of the early black medical doctors here in Annapolis, he gave me some kind of stuff, and I threw up half of the Chesapeake Bay. And I got some money that day! Everybody said, 'Brooks' daughter almost drowned.' 'You're the little girl who almost drowned? Oh, here, honey. Here's something for you.' I tried to go back in and jump and do it all over again." [116]

"The library was in Reynolds Tavern and it was on the way home from St. Mary's, and I would always go to the library and go to the children's room first. It wasn't too long before I had done the children's room, so Esther King let me go upstairs with the teenagers, and then I discovered the room way upstairs that had most of the poetry and literature. She was a great influence on me because she and my mother both instilled the love of reading and books and she would even let me sit out when an author would come and they'd have a little tea and things like that.

The library in those days was done by Dewey decimal system, which wasn't hard to learn. The front room had general fiction and newspapers and tables where you could sit and read. That was on the left-hand side coming through the front door and on the right-hand side, coming from the front door, was where you checked out and it was the office, and the little room right off of the office contained a lot of history and military history, Annapolis history. If you went straight through and downstairs on the lower level, it was the children's room. If you went upstairs, there was literature and reference.

There were always people in the library. There were always people that were there reading or there were ladies shelving books, and the library wasn't very big, but it was quiet. I would go there to read, visit my friends—the books—to check books out, and sometimes if I was all the way up top, I would sit in an alcove and write. It had nooks and crannies. I loved that library. Esther King was a hero—heroine, I guess." [117]

As with many aspects of life in Annapolis, the public libraries were segregated. The first public library opened in 1921 in the Assembly Rooms on Duke of Gloucester Street and later moved to Reynold's Tavern on Church Circle. It was not until 1940 that the black population had the same access to books at the library's Clay Street branch, pictured *above*. MdHR G 2140–84A

"We had nice teachers. Most of the teachers lived in this area. They lived down in the neighborhood. So these teachers were an example for the children, a model for the children. You know, they looked nice all the time going to school; they carried themselves nice. And you just figured, that's what I'm going to be when I grow up—I'm going to be like her. And I think that's the way the children felt, proud. They felt better inside, they knew they were somebody. They knew they could be somebody. And the parents instilled this in them. Regardless of what anybody thinks, you know what you can do.

I don't know whether integration helped or hurt. But I do know that these teachers who came and walked through this neighborhood and went out there to Bates every morning, they did a wonderful job with those children. Because they had heart and compassion. They tried to make them feel that they were somebody, they weren't just shoved in there because the law said so. They were in school because they wanted an education and they needed somebody to lead them. And they wanted the truth." [118]

"Monday night was bank night at the Star Theatre. The owner, Sam Eisenstein, used to give away, like, fifty dollars. And whoever got the winning ticket won the money. So bank night became a big thing; it was crowded in there.

In the theater there was a row in the center and rows on each side to get all the way up to the back. Each section of town had its own area where they sat. There was a section by the restrooms we called old folks' home, that meant where mothers and fathers and older people sat. And we had the front. There was a section for in-town, like Clay Street. Clay Street to downtown Annapolis—a lot of blacks lived in downtown Annapolis—up to where you hit that intersection where it starts Spa Road. That was Annapolis.

Spa Road sat in another section. Eastport sat in here. I mean, we didn't, obviously, fill up the whole section. But if you lived in Annapolis and you went to the Star Theatre and you were young, that was where you sat. If you live in Eastport, you sit there. And if you live in Spa Road, you'd need to sit over there. And Parole had a section." [119]

"Grandad used to have two little dogs. They were like people. He lived for those dogs. Those dogs never touched the ground. They stayed right on the bridge. They had a little doggy place where they went.

That house out on the bridge there had two rooms. Had one room like a living room or where you eat, and they had a bedroom in there, you know, two-bed bedroom. It was very small.

We had a toilet there. What it was was a little square house on the side of the bridge. If you went, you went in there. If that wind was blowing northwest, you made sure what you were going to do before you got in because there wasn't no bottom in the thing. You went right into the water.

At that time, they used to dump the sewage from the hospital up Spa Creek from where the bridge was. And we had this special little thing when we swam where we stuck our head out the water, done some doggy paddles like so that your head was about a foot above the water, and you could see what was coming so you could duck them. We learned to duck them dudes. They say it's unhealthy. You ought to see me now." [120]

Organizations from the Elks to the Booklovers' Club are woven throughout Annapolis' social fabric. For example, black employees at the Naval Academy formed the Blue and Gold Club, seen *above* c. 1945. MdHR G 2140–481

"There were no class boundaries. People who came from what was then probably the upper class of the blacks in Annapolis were associating with people who would be considered lower class. I mean, there was no class boundaries. People who were considered low class or from the lower class strata had their own homes because they worked at the United States Naval Academy and they had a constant income.

In those days, if a black man got married to anybody, he had to marry a schoolteacher. That was like marrying the Meyerhoff daughters or something. You had to marry a schoolteacher. I mean, that was the thing to do. Get a schoolteacher, man, and you've arrived. Because most of the women schoolteachers made more money than the men did. So it was good financially and it was also very secure. So my father, of course, married my mother because she was a schoolteacher!" [121]

Children of all ages and both races came out to frolic in the snow on Dean Street, c. 1946. MdHR G 2140–454

"I was raised here, well, I'll say the better part of my years, in this neighborhood. There were white children in the back. When I went out here in the morning, they all walked right straight through here and went to school the same way I did. But at that time, you did not walk with the white children. They weren't doing that, it was just unheard of. And you understood it. So you just went on about your business and they went about theirs. There was no friction there.

The thirties was some of the best time of my life. I knew what to expect of white people. I knew how they felt, so I accepted it. I could tolerate them because I knew what was inside and that was the main thing. Today children don't know now. And a lot of them, it hurts. It's better to know a person doesn't want to be bothered with you. Then you know how to treat them. But now, if they're going to pretend that they love you and then you meet them down Main Street and they turn their head, that's where the child gets hurt. And that's where all the animosity gets down in the craw. Sometimes it stays there. It makes a big difference in a child. And it all begins in childhood. Because when they're grown, they can see through it. But when they're children, it hurts." [122]

Being young and female in Annapolis usually meant spending time in the company of midshipmen. Weekend afternoons were set aside for sporting events and "pan-loes"— tea dances at Carvel Hall—and on Saturday nights there was usually a formal hop. *At left,* mids escaped from the academy to visit friends on Southgate Avenue, c. 1940. MdHR G 2140–387

"I worked at Carvel Hall in the fifties. I remember one day I toiled with a party—I served them and they played the slot machines out in the lobby. I think they were there like four or five hours and I'm still holding their check. And they were playing the slot machines in the lobby and then they'd come back and get another drink. And sometimes they'd take their drink and go back out there and play. And, 'Waitress, would you get me some change, please?' 'Some more change, please.' And they only left me seventy-five cents.

And they put a slew of money in the slot machines. I know they must have put in, I'd say, two or three hundred dollars in the machine. Eventually the machine got them." [124]

"When I was growing up in Annapolis, it was different with the midshipmen. It was a lot stricter then. A midshipman had to be a certain height, he had to have a clear complexion, his teeth had to be straight—it was really very strict at that time. Of course, there were no women, there were no blacks—it was difficult to get in.

They would come out into Annapolis. I don't know, I think there was a better relationship then because there wasn't as many of them and I think that they were more friendly and they didn't have the attitude like they're doing somebody a favor. I think that the midshipmen now have an attitude like you're here because we are, you're here to serve us. It wasn't that way then, it was a lot different.

I know of an episode last year—I ride the bus home—it was in the summer, it was hot, and I got on the bus to go home, and an elderly woman with a cane—I'd say she had to be in her seventies, at least— got on the bus and there were a lot of midshipmen on the bus. And none of them gave the woman their seat. I stood up and let her sit in my seat and I said, 'I apologize, ma'am.' I said, 'It takes an act of Congress to make them midshipmen. It would take an act of God to make them gentlemen.' And they all stood up! They were all very mad. Things have changed a lot." [123]

"Marcellus practically ran the working force of Carvel Hall when it came to banquets and the dining room and special parties." [125]

Marcellus Hall, *right,* began working at Carvel Hall on October 12, 1913, and he was still there when the hotel closed its doors in 1965. An enthusiastic tour guide as well as the bell captain, Marcellus had many friends among midshipmen as a result of his practice of calling anyone in a naval uniform "captain." MdHR G 1890–30,253

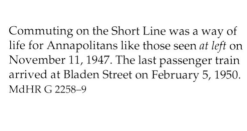

Commuting on the Short Line was a way of life for Annapolitans like those seen *at left* on November 11, 1947. The last passenger train arrived at Bladen Street on February 5, 1950.
MdHR G 2258–9

The Bladen Street station was demolished in 1957. For some years, one of the stops on the Short Line was the West Annapolis station, another was in Cedar Park.
MdHR G 2140–441

"The electric railroad was built before my time, around 1908. There had been steam rails before that. I guess the first railroad to come here was the Annapolis & Elkridge around 1840. Then in the 1880s, they built another line going up across the bridge called the Short Line.

The electric railroad was originally the Washington, Baltimore & Annapolis Railroad. It bought both of those lines and electrified them. There was a south shore line, which ran out West Street over the old Annapolis–Elkridge route to Odenton. Then the north shore line rolled over the old Short Line. That terminal was at Bladen Street. Up until the Depression, anyway, the trains departed for Baltimore a half-hour apart, from each station. So there was a train out to Baltimore every fifteen minutes. One man rode the south shore line, which terminal was at West Street, West Washington Street and Calvert Street. He rode the train which left at eight o'clock. He left his house about two to three minutes before eight o'clock and sort of ran, a sort of scamper-type of run, with an open overcoat in the winter. I think I'll always see him out there running. I guess they held the train for him if he didn't make it.

If you had to be in Baltimore for some reason or another and you planned to take a train out of the south shore station it would take about ten minutes to walk to the station from Southgate Avenue if you walked fast. But if you picked up your phone—there weren't any dial phones then, you had to go through an operator—you called a cab company. It was there across from the Bladen Street terminal. Not five minutes later that cab would get out to your house and get you back to Bladen Street and on that train.

And if it was two minutes of and it was too late to do that, if he got there right when the train was leaving, he'd run you out West Street and over Taylor Avenue to the West Annapolis stop, and get you on the train that way." [126]

139

Mary Baden and her daughters, Gloria and Barbara, posed at the family dinner table in 1947. Tom Baden's full-time employment was at the Naval Academy, but he moonlighted as a photographer. MdHR G 2140–456

"I led a very conventional life, with very conventional parents, in a very conventional situation, and there were not a lot of choices. My mother had dinner at one o'clock on Sunday, after you had been to church and Sunday school. Mother would put the roast in, we would go to church, we would come home, and we would have dinner. And we're talking a roast, and potatoes, and two vegetables, and a salad, and dessert, whether or not there was company." [127]

"In fact, back then, Clay Street was one of the elite streets in Annapolis. They had trees on the sidewalks going down, the most gorgeous houses. The blacks there really were mostly well-to-do blacks for back in these days. They owned their houses down there. It was a beautiful street. Everything that blacks had was right there. They didn't need to go anywhere else." [128]

"Just in the center of what you now call historic Annapolis, the Franklin Street area, the block between Church Circle and Cathedral Street, was more than half black and, indeed, there was a black church there until quite recently. And some of the finer black families of Annapolis lived there down on Shaw Street. What used to be the Fourth Ward, which was the Clay Street area, was, I suppose, what you'd call one hundred percent black in those days, but lots of the rest of Annapolis was not. If you look back in the historic records you'll see that free black people back even before the Civil War owned and occupied properties on Main Street, Duke of Gloucester, and all of these what you might call high-end neighborhoods now. They were perfectly free to build and buy and live where they pleased." [129]

A parade was the focus of attention for these Clay Street residents on a sunny day in 1948. MdHR G 1890–30,285

140

"I think Annapolis has lost a great deal. Annapolis, in my childhood and my formative years, was a mix of many kinds of people. In the Fourth Ward, off of West Street through Clay, between West Street and St. Anne's Cemetery, was the black area. And that area has mostly been torn down to make way for state and county buildings and a whole culture was lost there, and the same with the black area that was down on Pinkney and Fleet streets. When it got gentrified, all those people moved out.

I lived over in Spa View Heights. There was a farm next door. For years it was gardened by a black man who had horses, he plowed with the horse. Of course, in my generation, we all went to cowboy movies so we had great fantasies about the horse and not much fantasies about the man with the plow.

They raised tomatoes and cabbage and turnips, and he'd put them all in his wagon and take them around town and sell them. And it was a rural setting almost, because beyond Annapolis High, which is now Maryland Hall, was nothing but woods and streams. You could go over there and play in the woods and catch frogs, and crawfish still lived in the streams, and there was lots of wildlife, including lots of little boys.

On German Street, where I lived, the Ciccarones were Italian, the Gordons were Jewish, Mrs. Prymek and Mr. Prymek, who lived on the corner of Amos Garrett Boulevard, were from Czechoslovakia. It was like the League of Nations and people were accepting of all levels, you know. Mr. Tople was retired from the navy and had tattoos up and down his arms. He liked to sleep in a hammock in the backyard because it reminded him of the ships that he was on before World War II. And people seemed to be more accepting of the difference between neighbors, but now, you know, people like everybody to be pretty much the same and it's a more homogenized society." [130]

"I had been raised with the feeling that my mother's best friend, who lived three doors away from us, was always going to appear wherever I was in town. She was going to be at the drive-in with her family; she saw me holding hands with this fellow on State Circle, and my mother knew that night. There was a lot of that small town feeling, that you better be very careful what you do when you're out in public.

I remember my best friend and I would drive up Main Street, but she didn't want to wear her glasses because the guys were all hanging out at the pool hall. So my best friend, who could not see, was driving her convertible car up Main Street, and I was telling her who was standing outside the pool hall." [131]

143

Opening ceremonies for the celebration of the Annapolis Tercentenary, held in 1949, took place in Dahlgren Hall at the Naval Academy. MdHR G 1890–30,190A

"I remember Annapolis' Tercentenary as a really big deal. There were all kinds of events that I, as a kid, could go to or participate in. There was a pageant, I think over near Sandy Point on the old Labrot race track, there was a parade. I especially remember wearing a long dress and going with my mother to a garden party or something in the backyard of Reynold's Tavern, the old library. It was a beautiful sunny afternoon and there were all these people dressed up in colonial costumes, people I was used to seeing in regular clothes, but there they were in these lovely dresses and funny looking knee breeches, playing at being colonists.

I was really taken by the importance of this historical event. I remember lying in bed that night and wishing I could see the 400th anniversary celebration in 2049, and then realizing that I'd be more than a hundred years old then and knowing I'd never live that long. I guess that was the first time I really understood my own mortality. It was, and is still, a tremendous disappointment.

Of course, now that I've learned more about Annapolis history, and especially heard the stories of James Moss, who wrote *Providence, Ye Lost Towne at Severn*, I realize how funny the whole Tercentenary was. Annapolis wasn't founded in 1649 after all. Those first settlers came to Greenbury Point, not Spa Creek, and Annapolis didn't become a town until much later. Mr. Moss said he told the Tercentenary organizers all of this in 1949, but they went ahead anyhow. He spent more than thirty years researching the subject and finally published his book to prove he was right. And he was, but it was too late." [132]

"The man who came to town to do the Tercentenary had everybody in town dressed up as Pilgrims and on floats. We pulled together as a town—I think we need more of that. Now we seem to pull together for happy hour. I'm not sure that does it." [133]

The Tercentenary parade featured many elaborate floats. MdHR G 1890–30,189B

In the spring of 1949, William Labrot, Judge Benjamin Michaelson, and Chief of Police Will Curry conferred informally in front of the Courthouse. MdHR G 1890–30,151

"The chief of police, Will Curry, was an old-fashioned chief of police. He was not very tall but he wore a size twenty-two collar. I saw him with eight sailors from the *Reina Mercedes* one night when I was sweeping up in front of my grandfather's store on Main Street. I heard all this row down at the corner of Market Space and Green Street, so I asked my grandfather if I could go down and see what was going on. And he said I could but not to get into trouble.

So I walked down and there were eight sailors and Chief Curry. And Chief Curry was going to lock them up. They weren't about to let Chief Curry lock them up. The police station was up on Gloucester Street then, and they had the lock-up there. And so they were resisting stoutly, and he would grab first one and then the other and give them one whack, and down they would go and they did not get up. And in a very short period of time he whipped all eight of them, and it was not a fair fight—they couldn't do anything with him at all. And he had not even lost his cap. And so he gave them a few minutes to rest and then the ones who could get up carried the ones who couldn't, and he marched them up Green Street and he locked the whole bunch up.

And that was the first time I'd ever seen grownups fight, because the only thing I'd ever seen 'til then would be a little schoolyard scuffle. But that was no comparison. I must say he set a standard that I've seldom seen equaled since." [134]

"Cars were more available, and that was something different than the generation before. Kids were not only dating, but as soon as they were sixteen, they were allowed much more access to cars than anybody had had before. And there were drive-ins—drive-in food places and drive-in movies." [135]

Miss Airflyte presided over the new-model cars at the Annapolis Nash Company on October 22, 1948. MdHR G 1890–30,144D

Sunbathers sweltered on the beach at Bay Ridge on June 26, 1949, three years before the Chesapeake Bay bridge was opened. When access to the ocean was improved, the crowds began to migrate east and Bay beaches lost their appeal.
MdHR G 1890–30,181A

"I feel sometimes like we're rats in a cage, and you put too many rats in a cage and they get very strange. We are all becoming cornered rats. We are overpopulating, and it's very difficult for those of us who remember the years before, when there was quiet, and woods, and fields, and leisure, and slowness, and the seasons, and beaches. It is difficult, and I'm not that old, but I can remember that very, very well, and it does not exist now. Now you have asphalt, and noise, and people who are not as relaxed and easy as they used to be, and I call it 'the cornered-rat syndrome.'" [136]

St. John's College has revised its curriculum dramatically numerous times through its long history. In 1937, the college initiated a radical new program that concentrates on one hundred great books. *At right,* the historic Liberty Tree shades students in the spring of 1952. MdHR G 1890–28

"I learned about St. John's College because of the New Program. When I was in high school, I read an article that appeared in *Life* magazine, I believe in 1939, and simply fell in love with the idea. Well, I graduated and then I went off to war and I never thought about it after that. While I was in the service overseas, I remember explicitly, I was in the Philippines during a monsoon in a tent—a squad tent, large squad tent. And the tent had been pitched stupidly; we had made this encampment in a very boggy place. I think it might have been a rice paddy because water just flowed through it. One of the things that I found in the mud under my cot was a soggy old *Saturday Evening Post*. And the *Saturday Evening Post* had a story in it about St. John's College. And I said, 'That's where I want to go.'

Well, all of this was a bit of an omen, I think, so when I came home in early 1946—in fact, I was discharged on New Year's Day, 1946—I set about applying to colleges. St. John's College was my first choice. St. John's embraced me with open arms. I realized later they were desperate for students!

So I came to the school of my first choice in 1946. And this was just at the surge of the veterans coming. And my class was—oh, I don't know how big it was, but more than half of us were veterans. It was a strange situation. The majority of the freshman class were veterans, and we were older than the seniors, by far. Because at that time St.

John's College had hung on during the war with early admissions. That is to say, they admitted youngsters, promising kids, who hadn't graduated from high school. So there were kids, who had been admitted as freshmen at sixteen, who would be nineteen-year-old seniors, and here we were, twenty-one, twenty-two, and sort of hardened veterans, seeming much older than these young seniors. It was a strange, inverted time.

My first day at St. John's College, after dinner, a group of us brand-new friends went down to the foot of Prince George Street. I believe it was where the old ferry slip used to be. By then, the ferry had been already moved out to Sandy Point, where later the bridge was built. It was very picturesque and quaint and rundown and not a yacht in sight that I can remember, but a lot of workboats. It was a very rough—it was not beautiful, but it was picturesque. The harbor I would describe as a picturesque place with its own kind of rough beauty but not the kind of sleek high-rises, I mean, these overwhelming high-rises and fancy restaurants and sleek yachts that you see down there now. It was just a working waterfront, very picturesque, though.

And it was at sunset and I remember I was swept by a feeling of yearning. And I said, aloud, 'I wish I had been born here.' It was a very sentimental, highly charged moment. And then we went back up to the college and life went on." [137]

On September 2, 1952, an expectant crowd awaited Clarabell the Clown, star of "The Howdy Doody Show," at Frank Slama's shoe store, 55 West Street.
MdHR G 1890–30,212A

"We were the first ones, I think, in Annapolis to get a television set, and all the kids on this street used to come here and watch Howdy Doody. When Sam would come home from the store, he'd have to walk in front of them, and all the kids would get really upset. They didn't want him walking in front of them, because they would miss something.

Television was like a miracle. My mother thought that was a crazy thing to put your money in. Why buy it? She was mad when we bought this television set, and, lo and behold, it wasn't very long before she bought one for herself." [138]

Sam Snyder seemed to be fighting a losing battle as he shoveled snow in front of his tailor shop on Maryland Avenue, c. 1953. The serenity of this scene would be lost as soon as the snow melted and people ventured out of doors again. MdHR G 1890–545

"I liked the town quality of Annapolis. It was just across the street which made it very nice. You could go downtown for cigarettes or for beer or for milk shakes. And those were my chief preoccupations in those days—drinking beer, eating ice cream, and going to the movies. The Little Campus was much more of a soda fountain, and there was a place next door called the G&J.

The G&J was all pink and blue with big leather banquettes, very garish with fluorescent lights overhead. And very comfortable but not at all cozy. Nice, big, sort of leatherette banquettes around formica-topped tables. We could have hamburgers and beer there, or hamburgers and ice cream. Hamburgers and milk shakes. And we would sit there and smoke cigarettes and drink beer and philosophize a lot.

Most of us didn't get much beyond the G&J, or Maryland Avenue. There was a place across the street called Davis', I believe. Mr. Davis was a stationer and he sold out-of-town newspapers. And even then you could get the *New York Times* and a *Wall Street Journal*, and you weren't just stuck with the *Evening Capital* or the Baltimore *Sun* or the *Washington Post*. I remember getting not just newspapers but interesting magazines. You could buy things like *Fortune* magazine and *The New Republic* and *Nation*, that sort of thing." [139]

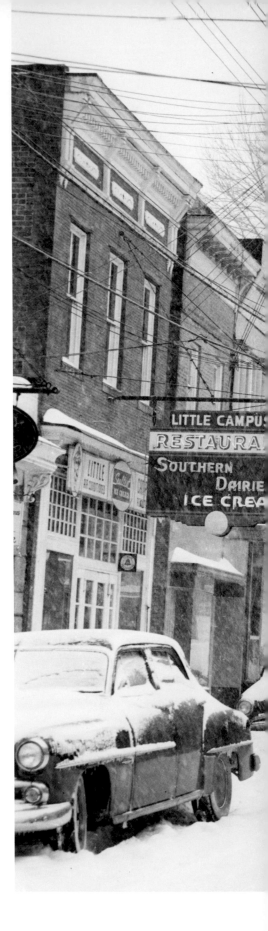

153

The Easter egg hunt at the State House, *at right* c. 1951, the Christmas parade, and the New Year's Day open house at the Governor's Mansion were annual rites observed by many Annapolitans. MdHR G 1890–30,239A

"We had an Easter parade on State Circle. I can remember that because the boy that I was going steady with at that time and I won Mr. and Mrs. Teenage, whatever that was.

My mother thought that junior high was promoting dating and promoting this kind of going steady and pulling the kids away from the parents and trouble, trouble, trouble right here in River City. It was a difficult time for parents because I think they had a little more control in the thirties and forties, and I think my generation was just starting to see the rise of the 'ugly teenager,' with money, too, as a consumer. People were starting to try to sell to the teenager products and clothing and a look and whatever we were doing, hula hoops and all that kind of stuff." [140]

155

The Girls' Service Organization at the armed services YMCA on Northwest Street attempted to provide a home away from home for black service personnel stationed in the Annapolis area, especially during the holidays. MdHR G 2140–287

"Black people then understood what the rules of the game were, as did the white families. There was this kind of acknowledgement that existed. And because everybody had been 'brought up carefully,' as the song says in *South Pacific*, they knew what was expected of them. I knew the buses were segregated and the theaters were segregated.

I did see one confrontation, later on, after I left the service and I was in a bar down on Main Street. I was sitting in the bar. And there was a black guy, you know, sitting at the bar. And we were talking. And as the evening wore on, it seemed that some people in the bar took exception to him being there. And while there were words being said, there weren't any fights. But they didn't want that black guy there and they made it quite clear in their language that he was intruding by coming into a white bar. He said, 'How come I can't come in here? I've been in the war and I've fought for my country. And I can't even come in here and get a drink.' It's really sad. But that's about the only direct experience I can recall having with a situation like that." [141]

The Weekenders was an informal social club that gathered regularly in the early 1950s. The Hynsons, Badens, Williams, Allens, Wisemans, and Browns were among the members who met in each other's homes on Saturday nights. MdHR G 2140–449

"Knowledge and understanding made a big difference. I feel that the black race of people were determined to raise themselves up, especially economically. They wanted nice houses, they wanted nice clothes, they wanted nice places for their children to go, they wanted segregation to end in schools, and they worked toward that goal. They allowed people to know that, 'I can socialize with you, I can walk on your same level and not be a pain or a nuisance to you. The same as I don't want you to be one to me.' And they strived toward that goal.

Right here in Annapolis, you think of the uneducated people who sent four and five and six and seven children to college. That got out in the fields and plowed and made money to send those children to school, to college, and they didn't have education worth a dime. But they were determined that it would not be that way with their children. We had a fellow used to live there on Fleet Street, he wound up being a doctor. It was a matter of being determined to advance. You have to just stay and fight at one level, and they did it." [142]

Elizabeth, Queen Mother of England, visited on November 8, 1954. Governor Theodore R. McKeldin joins her as she greets the crowd on State Circle. MdHR G 2140–355

"The Queen Mother came to Annapolis. I was at the academy then in the English, history and government department. I didn't go to the parade, but when it was time for her to go, I just went down the back stairs and across our parking lot, and when she and the admiral drove by, I waved to her, and she waved to me." [143]

"I was active with the Chamber of Commerce in the early fifties, and we had a running argument with the city council about parking meters. The council claimed that the meters were being installed to 'help' us by keeping the traffic moving so people wouldn't park in the same spot all day long. They said that it would benefit local merchants. We said it was simply for revenue collection. The fine was a buck in those days.

So one Saturday morning I looked out the window of my studio at 5 State Circle and saw a cop giving a ticket to the only car on the circle. Obviously he wasn't worried about the turnover of parking spaces. I climbed out on the roof and made this photograph, which we displayed at the Chamber of Commerce. I don't know that it did any good, but I thought it made a statement." [144]

Parking tickets have long been the bane of drivers in Annapolis. In 1954, this policeman wrote a ticket to the lone car overparked at a meter—a Rolls Royce. MdHR G 1890–552

"After Sam lost everything two or three times, he fell overboard and nearly drowned, and that woke him up. That's what he always told me. That put him on the wagon. Then in 1941, he opened up Sam's on Dock Street. He'd buy crabs off of me and pay me for steaming them, and he'd put them on the bar for a quarter apiece. A quarter apiece. He'd have sandwiches for a nickel or dime, and hard-boiled eggs for a nickel. He was the cheapest place in town. You could get twelve-ounce cans of Munich beer for fifteen cents, and a shot of bar whiskey and a chaser for a quarter.

The oystermen would come in there, the crabbers would come in there, the streetsweepers would come in there, the admirals, the senators, the congressmen. Everybody would come see Sam." [145]

Sam Lorea's Tavern at 136 Dock Street is legendary. *Below*, Gene Griscom and Spike Webb pose with Sam on October 19, 1954. MdHR G 2140–393

"They took the people's houses and gave them, in my opinion, a pittance for what they were worth. They couldn't duplicate what they had for the money that they gave them. They had no places to go. My grandfather and grandmother were in their eighties, and if it hadn't been for my aunt having a house in Eastport, they'd have had no place to go.

The sad part about it, the government took that in 1941, and tore the houses down, and it laid empty until 1954, when they started the field house. So for thirteen years, they did nothing, just left the empty land there for thirteen years." [146]

"The watermen were early risers every day. Long hours of the day, usually until nightfall, they would be on the water, whether it was fishing or oystering. They went out there under any weather conditions, except when they couldn't move. They would stay out there until they got as much of the supply as they could possibly get because it was worth practically nothing. If the market was gutted, they would only get a few cents a pound for fish or, say, oysters. Practically you couldn't give them away at certain times of the year." [147]

Above, this view taken from the dome of the Naval Academy chapel, c. 1954, shows that, although the navy seized several blocks in the Hell Point neighborhood in 1941, no significant use was made of the land for more than a decade.
MdHR G 1890–114B

Left, the oyster fleet at City Dock, c. 1955.
MdHR G 1890–30,199

161

Neighborhood churches, like St. Luke's Church in Eastport, *left* c. 1955, were often adjuncts to larger parishes. Reverend James Smiley (on the steps, wearing a hat) and his entire congregation spilled out of St. Luke's for this portrait. Roger "Pip" Moyer, later mayor of Annapolis, stands under the window on the left. MdHR G 1890–30,242A

"I always remember Sunday school classes at St. Luke's, which was down in Eastport at Second Street and Chesapeake Avenue, before it was where it is now. The Reverend Smiley, who was a true holy man, never married and he lived very humbly. What little bit he made he gave to the poor. He lived in one room over on Prince George Street. But as he walked around town the Eastport people would just follow him like the pictures you see of Jesus. It was almost like the man had a blessing on him and would bestow that blessing to you. You just felt so good when you were around him.

Oh, he was something. And a brilliant human being. A very small man, about 5'1" or 5'2" tall. But he just had a quality about him that you just don't see in humans. A true holy man. You know, like you think of the holy men of India and the Far East and all. He had that mysticism about him. And not a kook. Very practical. Just an exceptional person.

I remember when he would lead us over every Christmas and every Easter to St. Anne's Church. But it was known that we really weren't, socially, the equal of St. Anne's Church. Because they had a roped-off section for us when we got there. And on Easter we were given a little plant to take back with us." [148]

163

Davis' was a family-owned and operated restaurant and tavern. Located at 400 Chester Avenue, it was a favorite haunt for the black population of Eastport. MdHR G 2140–479

"One thing I do remember about Eastport is the way the black and the white people got along over there. And when I took Alex Haley through there in the sixties—when he was doing his research on the book, *Roots*, and all, and we were talking—he said, in his entire travels in the United States he had never seen better race relations.

One of the reasons, I think, is because the people live next door to each other. You'd go to areas of Eastport, even back in the thirties, where you had a black family living next to a white family, then another black family, then another white family. In other words, the salt and pepper neighborhoods mixture. The common denominator was—everybody made their living off the water. So the color of your skin didn't mean any more than the size of your shoes. We were all human beings." [149]

During June Week and Parents' Weekend, local restaurants were filled to capacity. The rest of the time most eating establishments were sparsely populated, as the Cruise Inn at 66 State Circle was, *above*, in 1955. Annapolitans usually ate at home, and the great surge of tourists had not yet begun.
MdHR G 1890–30,141A

"When I was here as a student, the restaurant situation was never very good. It was not much better when I returned. The Cruise Inn was still there. I always saw that as a Methodist place, wonderful food and no wine." [150]

"My parents used to buy all their meats from Rookie's. At that time Rookie's was located on West Street in the block between Monticello and Southgate. It was a very small store and it was right on our way home, so we would stop there and pick up that night's groceries. We were never organized enough to shop a week ahead of time.

So Rookie's was a very important part of our lives and we knew everyone who worked there. I remember one year at Christmas, we were supposed to go to my aunt's house in Alexandria, but I got really sick and we couldn't go. So on Christmas morning my parents called Rookie, and he went down to the store and got a turkey and brought it to the house. I can't imagine that kind of service today.

Rookie actually lived on the same street we did—South Cherry Grove Avenue. One of our neighbors had a very large garden, and I can remember this one evening sitting at their picnic table, and there were a whole bunch of adults there as well as kids. We were shelling peas.

Two things I remember that happened that night. The man who owned the garden found a turtle in his tomato patch, and he threw that turtle against a big tree and smashed it to smithereens right in front of everybody. None of the adults responded at all, but I was horrified. To me turtles were pets.

Then he came back and sat down and continued shelling peas, and they all started talking about the fact that Rookie was going to be moving downtown to Market Space and taking over the old Community

166

Once considered the outskirts of town, by 1955, about when the photograph *at left* was taken, the West Street area near Monticello Avenue was regarded as Annapolis proper. The A&P was on the corner, and Rookie's Meat Market was practically next door. MdHR G 1890–30,268B

Market building. It seemed like they talked about it forever. It was a very long and involved conversation among the adults, and the gist of it was that Rookie was crazy. There was no way in the world that he would be able to survive in downtown Annapolis. Everybody was leaving downtown. The shopping center was opening up and all the stores were at that point either opening up branches at Parole, or else they were just closing up altogether from lack of business.

Obviously downtown was dying, and here was crazy Rookie making a giant leap of faith and taking his little tiny store there. You could have taken six or eight of his old store and put them in the Market Space store—it was that big a change in the style of store he was going to be running. A couple of the people who were there were bankers, and my guess is that they were either helping to finance him or had turned him down, but I think they knew quite a bit about the business end of this, and they just thought he was nuts.

Even to this day, when I go into Rookie's, I smile and think that Rookie was smarter than all of them put together. He sure knew what he was doing. And it also makes me think that that man was wrong about smashing the turtle, too." [151]

"Parole was sparsely populated, with one black school—I think it was a three-room school—several churches, of course, black churches. The railroad came from Annapolis through Parole en route to Baltimore, and there was a railroad station on West Street. Transportation in the area was either a cab or the little trolley—dinky, I called it—going into the city. Making a couple of stops, it took about ten, fifteen minutes to get to Annapolis. It didn't take very long. But, for the most part, people used, if they didn't have cars, and I didn't have one at that time, they used taxicabs

Although Parole was still a relatively quiet neighborhood, the intersection at West Street extended and Solomons Island Road was already dangerous, as evidenced by the scene *above*, c. 1955. MdHR G 1890–30,210A

to get in and out of the city or anyplace else they wanted to go.

There was one cab company in Parole, owned by the Harrington family. Now, I don't recall if there were others. I just don't recall that. But he had quite a route. He ran all around Parole and Annapolis. So he took care of most of the traffic that had to go in and out of the city." [152]

167

Of all the boatyards that lined the shores around Annapolis, Trumpy's, located on Spa Creek in Eastport, was the most famous. During World War II the facility was known as the Annapolis Yacht Yard. PT boats and sub-chasers were constructed there and tested nearby. Later John and Donald Trumpy bought the yard and made it famous for the production of luxury yachts like this one, c. 1955. MdHR G 1890–557A

"I was actually the first generation of the family that didn't make part of their living off the water. All my uncles had the combination of a good government job or at Trumpy's, where there was a lot of stability in health benefits, and then worked on the water on the side.

And in those days watermen never reported income. What you made in catch you ate or sold and it was yours. God put it there. You harvested it. And it belonged to you by the sweat of your brow.

These people ended up very independent financially, most of them, because they lived very frugally, and they saved their money and invested in real estate in Eastport.

All summer you could hear 'clink, clink, clink.' It was the sound of summer. And that was the caulking hammer. Boats would come open at the seams, the old wooden boats, and quite often they had to caulk them and then put red lead over it and then copper. And that would keep them from leaking for the summer. You would hear that through Eastport, along Trumpy's and stuff. That was the sound of summer.

But it's fiberglass now, and it's just not the same. It's not part of us. It is good to see them working and all, and the sails up on some of the boats, and stuff like that. But fiberglass boats don't do anything for me." [154]

Elwood Jones, *above* c. 1955, began his career as a butcher working for Mac Peterson in the Market House. After the Market House was renovated in 1972, Woody became the first black merchant to operate a stall there. MdHR G 2140–22A

"If you went into a store that had no seats, you were almost treated like anybody else. It's almost ironic, because we had a market downtown— the same market that's been remodeled—anybody could go in there, any color could go in there. You could stand next to this one, you could stand next to that one, because there were no seats. It was one of the most ridiculous things. Anybody could go to the oyster house because they had no seats. You could go into any grocery store. You could go into any clothes store because they had no seats. There seemed to be a policy, there seemed to be some type of an unwritten law, we can work together, we can talk together, but we draw the line at association together." [153]

Carr's Beach was the most popular black resort for miles around. Located on the Annapolis Neck peninsula where the Severn River meets the Chesapeake Bay, Carr's Beach drew enormous crowds from Baltimore, Washington, and beyond. Attractions included swimming, amusements, rides, and best of all, big-name entertainment. MdHR G 2140–219

"Carr's Beach was just nothing but good times. The best entertainers in the world came down to Carr's Beach. From Sarah Vaughn to James Brown, Ike and Tina Turner, Dinah Washington, the Drifters.

I had a white guy that said, 'Peggy, I couldn't get in Carr's Beach.'

I said, 'You know what, I couldn't get in Bay Ridge either.'" [155]

"Carr's Beach was the only place in the summertime that blacks could go and see major acts—Fats Domino, James Brown—really top acts. And they used to have night beach parties, and also Sunday beach parties. I remember when Fats Domino was down there once, there were so many cars going into the beach that the cars were backed all the way to what is now known as

Parole Shopping Center. It was that many cars. Insofar as blacks were concerned, it was a black Coney Island. And Fats Domino, or Sam and Dave, or Otis Redding or somebody would come down and it would be packed down there. It was like being in a mass of humanity.

Going there from Annapolis, we were kind of like 'PCs,' privileged characters. The policemen all were special policemen, and George Phelps ran it. George had this big white stick we used to call the rod of correction, and they had a little jail where they would lock people up. Most of the time, they would lock up guys from Washington and Baltimore because they would always come down there and get drunked up. And most of the time, any of us who got in fights with any of these guys from out of town, we'd never get locked up.

Sparrow's Beach was a smaller rendition of Carr's. You could go either to Carr's or Sparrow's. But people would go to Sparrow's to be laid back and have a picnic. Sparrow's Beach was a small beach and didn't have the big acts.

A lot of whites would come there. White people would come to Carr's

Hoppy Adams was an ever-present personality at Carr's Beach. A popular disk jockey, Hoppy emceed most events, like this beauty contest in 1953 that took place at Carr's Beach. MdHR G 2140–220

The throngs returned week after week. Although Carr's Beach technically was segregated, occasionally there were white blues fans in audiences like the one *at right* in August 1956. MdHR G 2140–154

Beach and have a good time. When Joe Louis fought for his championship once or twice, he would train down there. He was this gigantic man who was heavyweight champion of the world, and he was sitting there punching a bag. I guess it was because it was down by the water and it was calm, so he was training down there during the week for a championship fight.

During the week, Monday through to Wednesday, Thursday, or Friday, people would just come down there to picnic. It wasn't crowded at all, there were no bands there or anything. In the summer from Thursday right straight on through Sunday, it was like thousands of people. And they had stands where you could throw stuff and knock down dolls.

I remember there was a fence back there and once someone found a dead snake somewhere off in the swamp, and he came in and threw that sucker in there and they took that fence down. I mean, blacks are habitually scared of snakes—everybody is. And somebody threw that black snake in the air, and it was like a 'whoosh' and they went 'wham!,' and the thing just came down.

You could dance in the back part. That's where the kids from Annapolis were. We were dancers, so we could hang out back here and dance and boogie and carry on. Now on Saturday night there was a little more room unless it was a real big show, like Fats Domino or something. But Sundays it was always crowded. It was awesome. Just to be able to get that close to a Sam and Dave or Fats Domino, it was outstanding." [156]

Annapolis Roads Country Club featured a
swimming pool, seen *above* on June 6, 1955,
and a golf course just across the road. This
clubhouse, like its more elaborate predecessor, was destroyed by fire.
MdHR G 1890–30,282B

"My parents used the country club as
summer day care. My memory is
that we were dropped off first thing
in the morning and picked up last
thing at night. We lived on the hot
dogs and peanut butter crackers at
the snack bar. It's a wonder we're
still alive." [157]

Until relatively recently, much of the land surrounding Annapolis was in agricultural use. The Bowie farm, *above*, was still using horse-drawn equipment to havest the tobacco crop c. 1956. The Annapolis Cove community occupies the site today.
MdHR G 1890–14

"There were people doing active farming on Bay Ridge Road in the 1950s and 1960s. The Bowie farm always raised tobacco and corn, and now it grows houses; this whole county is growing houses. It bothers me because we have lost the quality of life that people came here for and it is killing the goose that laid the egg. And a dead goose is really pretty unattractive." [158]

Although the automobile parked on Church Circle suggests otherwise, this scene was photographed on June 21, 1957. The car was an official vehicle of the Parking Meter Department of the City of Annapolis. MdHR G 1890–30,148

Brewer Hill Cemetery on West Street has been the final resting place for many of Annapolis' black community for more than a century. *Below,* c. 1955, a visitor lingers among the graves. MdHR G 2140–406

"When I was a young fellow, on the weekends, when people came to town to shop, the first block of West Street from Church Circle to Cathedral Street for a period of thirty years was the most prosperous block in all of Anne Arundel County. There were no stores from here to Baltimore. There was nothing from Annapolis down to southern Maryland. So all the farmers, everybody, had to come to town to shop on the weekends. And when it came to weekends, Friday and Saturday, you couldn't walk up the sidewalks."

[159]

"My grandfather was Charles Phelps, and he was among the original twelve people who purchased the land for the cemetery from Judge Nicholas Brewer, putting twenty dollars down for $784. Later on Wiley H. Bates became the secretary of the Brewer Hill Cemetery for Colored People of Anne Arundel County.

The cemetery was started in 1884, but our research has shown us that Nicholas Brewer had allowed blacks to be buried there before it was an official cemetery. There were slaves buried there.

Judge Nicholas Brewer was white—that's who the land was bought from. Brewer Avenue was named for him." [160]

Hurricane Hazel conjures up dramatic memories for those who experienced its violence. Hazel hit Annapolis in October 1954 and caused extensive damage. *Above*, Dock Street, next to City Dock, sustained some of the worst flooding.
MdHR G 2238–15G

"I remember Hurricane Hazel. In Hurricane Hazel, the water was two feet high. What we did, we'd tape the doors and the windows, and we'd take boat caulking and a caulking gun and go around it. And in Hurricane Hazel, we had that much water up against our building, but none in the store. The only water came in the store was from the pressure that pushed down on the storm drains and pushed water up through the floor drains. A&P didn't lose a penny. Some of them did, but we didn't." [161]

"Historic Annapolis was just about two years old when we learned that Carroll the Barrister was going to be demolished in lieu of a new office building that was to go there. We didn't have any experience in raising any money. We could not ourselves raise sufficient money to buy the house and lot, which, if I remember correctly, was seventy-five thousand dollars.

Carroll the Barrister was obviously an extremely fine house from an

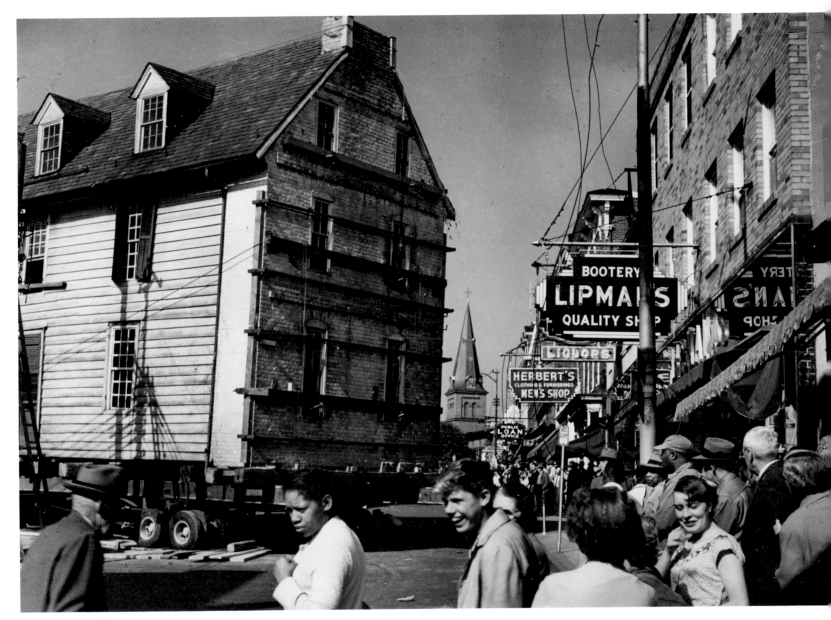

architectural point of view, and also because of its association with Charles Carroll the Barrister, who wrote the Maryland Declaration of Rights. He was supposed to have been born there.

It had been purchased by Mr. Greenfield, who owned Peerless on Main Street. Things were different then, because we had so many local people on the board of Historic Annapolis who, of course, did business with Mr. Greenfield. They all got

very busy and met with Mr. Greenfield, and he agreed that he would give Historic Annapolis the house if we would move it. We didn't want to move it, but there seemed no other solution.

It took two days to move it. They divided it into two sections and they started up the street. Mr. Lazenby was in insurance, and they got it about in front of where Café Normandie is, and Mr. Lazenby asked the man who was moving it what kind of

The move of the Carroll the Barrister House was the cynosure of life in Annapolis on October 3–4, 1955. The town turned out to watch the historic home inch away from its original location at the corner of Main and Conduit streets, *above*, and make its way to St. John's College campus.   MdHR G 2238–1P

insurance he had. He said he had none, he was a Seventh Day Adventist and he believed in the Lord. Mr. Lazenby made considerable speed to his office and put insurance on it." [162]

179

Santa Claus was almost lost in the crowd that gathered in Eastport to see the annual Christmas parade at Sixth Street and Severn Avenue c. 1955.   MdHR G 1890–30,218A

"We made such a great big thing over Christmas because we always were together—whole families were always together. Families were so different then than they are today.

When we built this house, I insisted that everybody who worked on it be from Eastport. I have never lived further than three miles from where I was born. Instead of having blood in my veins, I have salt water. I am addicted to this place." [163]

"The houses connected on Larkin Street. They were clean, very clean—that's the one thing I remember about my childhood. I don't ever remember going to anybody's house that was dirty. Even in the projects over on Clay Street, which is now College Creek Terrace, it was very clean. If a kid did something bad in this town in those days, it was a major scandal, if a black kid did something." [164]

The houses on Larkin Street, *right*, c. 1955, were demolished about 1970. The street was renamed City Gate Lane. MdHR G 2140–401

Although the Supreme Court ruled against segregation in schools in 1954, resistance was strong among administrators, and it took some years before Anne Arundel County schools were fully integrated. In 1957, *above*, Adams Park was still completely black. MdHR G 2140–450

"I don't know anything more rewarding than to be teaching something and see a child's mind unfold and accept or see what it is that you're doing. There's just something about that that makes teaching worthwhile, I think." [166]

Religious education was an influential aspect in the lives of many young Annapolitans. These young men attended Hebrew school at Kneseth Israel Synagogue, c. 1955. MdHR G 2266–1

"There was a two-floor synagogu[e] there, and after school I would hurry up home as a little boy fro[m] about age nine, I would think, e[ight] or nine, and I would go to Hebr[ew] school every day. And the rabbi[s] there waiting to teach us. They [had] two or three different classes, a[nd] we would be taught to read Hebrew, translate, and such. I remember it very well because [I] have to go to Hebrew school u[p]

"About '27 or '28, Charlie Chance decided that Annapolis needed what is known as a marina now—a facility for yachts, good facilities. Up until that time, a first-class yacht could find no acceptable docking area in the town. They used to come in, they used to lay at anchor, and they'd have the tenders or their launches or the dinghy to bring the people ashore. Mostly in those days, the yachts were so big they had the launches that came in and dropped the people off into the town.

So Chance decided that a marina—they called it a yacht basin—was necessary. He started this construction and he bought all the properties from where the old Spa Creek bridge was and the yacht club to the beginning of the entrance to the City Dock. So he bought all that property there that included the ice house, McNasby's, and Sarles'. Ben Sarles had a marine engine shop and he repaired boats there, right next to McNasby's. Also, he bought the Knights of Columbus hut, which sat on a little island in the middle of the harbor there, on oyster shells.

The hut sat on oyster shells. I suspect it was one of McNasby's dumping places for his oyster shells that built this little island that the hut was built on. It had quite a long—several hundred feet, 150 feet or maybe 200 feet—causeway that reached from the shoreline to the hut. And this hut was where the Knights of Columbus held their meetings and did all their activities.

This would have to be in the twenties, round about '28, I'd say. Before he completed the project, Wall Street crashed and the Depression began. Well, that knocked his project into a cockeyed situation and he couldn't finish it. So when the Roosevelt administration came in, they set up the Reconstruction Finance Corporation and lent Chance the money to finish this project out. So he completed the yacht basin there.

The next thing that happened was that he did not have the traffic to support the complex, and he did not have the business that he thought he was going to have in building yachts. With the Depression and all, no one was buying yachts; no one was really using the waterways for recreational purposes around this way at all. So he went bankrupt.

Then he lost the yacht basin, and the Reconstruction Finance Company reclaimed it and they offered the yacht basin to the city of Annapolis. They turned it down. Then a private organization set up and bought it from the Reconstruction Finance, using the yacht club as the figurehead for the purchase of it because the Reconstruction Finance could not sell directly to private enterprise. They had to sell it to either a community or to a nonprofit organization. So that's how the yacht basin got started there."
[167]

185

Eastport also attracted the interest of developers. The Duckett farm, *below* c. 1960, would soon have hundreds of apartments and a shopping center squeezed onto its acreage. MdHR G 1890–30,284A

Until the mid 1960s, local farmers roamed the streets of Annapolis hawking fresh fruits and vegetables. Still others did a brisk business outside the Market House. MdHR G 1890–30,197

"When we built our store on the corner of Bay Ridge and Chesapeake in 1951, I would watch the people at the farm across the street. I would watch the man driving the tractor. His wife sat on the back, and she would stick the tobacco plants in the earth. It was typically farmland, really. And it was perfectly lovely." [175]

"All of what is now the Eastport Shopping Center was the Duckett's farm, and I went past that mailbox every morning of my life, down Chesapeake Avenue, and their mailbox was right at the corner of Bay Ridge Avenue and Chesapeake Avenue. They had a mailbox with a

duck on it and 'E T T.' I must have passed that mailbox a thousand times before I was old enough to realize that it meant Duckett.

There was a road that went from the mailbox up to an old farmhouse, which stood in the middle of what is now apartments and fields on either side—big cultivated fields." [176]

"Anne Arundel County got very famous in Baltimore and the surrounding areas so that for everything that they hawked on the street and that the A-rabs sold in Baltimore they would say, 'Anne Arannel tomatoes,' 'Anne Arannel' this and 'Arannel' that. Even, 'Anne Arannel oranges.'" [177]

Epilogue

"One spring day, the sun was shining, it was warm. I had cabin fever, so I left the office, went on down and sat on the dock. And, of course, there were lots of other people down there. And I'm enjoying the ducks and the sunshine and so on and Billy Phelps comes by. And Billy is an Annapolitan, lived on Shipwright Street, and Billy has a loud voice, nice guy, good singing voice, too. He said, 'Tom, how the hell are you?'

I said, 'I'm fine, Bill, how are you doing?'

He said, 'I'm doing all right. But, you know, I don't live around here anymore.'

I said, 'You don't?'

He said, 'No, there's too many foreigners.' He said, 'I've moved up to Spa Road.' All the foreigners looked at us. And he said, 'Yeah, you know, it's not fit to go downtown anymore.' He says, 'Nothing but foreigners.' He says, 'Don't know anybody. All these people roll in from Baltimore and Washington and Georgetown and this sort of thing.'

A lot of the old-time Annapolitans, I think, sort of feel that way. A couple of years ago I was walking down Main Street to get the morning paper, and this truck pulled up. The window rolls down and this boy says, 'Christ, they killed me, Tom.' See, that's an old Annapolis expression. 'Just look at this town,' he says. 'You could shoot a cannon down Main Street,' he says. 'You wouldn't hit a single Annapolitan and you'd wipe out half of Georgetown! Business is good, but Christ, they killed me. You could go up and down Main Street three or four times and never see a single soul you know.'

The town is like a stage set. It's beautiful, the lovely old homes are beautiful, but the actors are gone. And this is really too bad. The local people have accepted too many offers that they couldn't refuse, and they've gone elsewhere. And the great people that knitted together the fabric of the lovely old town are just no longer here. It's rare that you see anybody that you know downtown anymore. And I think that the percentage of what my grandmother used to call transients—my grandfather was a transient—he was born in Dorchester County in 1867, moved to Annapolis in 1876, died at nearly 104 and he was a transient because he wasn't born in Annapolis—but I think when you get past a certain percentage of people who come to an area from elsewhere, you sort of lose the town's integrity." ■ [183]

Aerial with City Dock in foreground, May 28, 1965. MdHR G 1890–1954A

Bibliography

Throughout its history, Annapolis has caught the interest of many gifted writers. The themes they developed and the clues they dropped were the starting point for much of the research for this book. I am particularly indebted to Ann Jensen for her thoughtful articles on Annapolis' ethnic groups that have appeared in *Annapolitan* magazine over the years. She was also helpful in suggesting potential narrators for oral history interviews. Roxanna White Kieffer offered a gold mine of information in her newspaper articles for the Baltimore *Sun* and *Evening Sun* about life in Annapolis during the 1930s. The sensitivity and elegance of her prose provided an inspirational role model. Another fertile source was the extensive scrapbook collection assembled by the late Dutch Britton. More than fifty years of newspaper clippings supplied facts and figures, as well as ideas for other potential sources. I am grateful to his widow, Beatrice Britton, for permitting me to explore this rich repository of Annapolis history.

Tom Worthington contributed one of the most valuable records: the 1941 assessment made of the Hell Point property absorbed by the Naval Academy. This fascinating document contains not only a wealth of statistical and sociological information, but also a wonderful cache of photographs of every structure that was demolished by the navy. It should be noted that the pictures, some of which appear in this book, were taken by Tom himself, then twelve years old.

City directories and telephone books were helpful in locating businesses at specific addresses, thus helping to date photographs. Mayors' reports and census information contain statistics that document the steady growth and gradual changes in the character of the town.

Extensive browsing in old editions of the Annapolis *Evening Capital* and the Baltimore *Sun* and *Evening Sun* revealed abundant information beyond significant daily events. The terminology used and the attention, or lack thereof, paid to certain stories provided insight into the concerns and attitudes of the day.

Several secondary sources were particularly useful in probing the longstanding and significant relationship between Annapolis and its two institutions of higher learning. Tench Francis Tilghman's *The Early History of St. John's College in Annapolis*, J. Winfree Smith's *A Search for the Liberal College*, and Jack Sweetman's *The U. S. Naval Academy: An Illustrated History* are excellent books on their subjects.

The files accumulated during research for *Then Again . . . Annapolis, 1900–1965* may be found at the Maryland State Archives in collection MdHR G 2140. Most of the books listed in the bibliography are available at the archives, the Maryland State Law Library, or the Maryland Department at the Enoch Pratt Free Library in Baltimore.

Alphabetical Directory of the City of Annapolis. 1934.

Annapolis City Directory. Annapolis: Gould and Halleron, 1910.

Annapolis Telephone Directory. Baltimore: Chesapeake and Potomac Telephone Co. of Baltimore City, 1932.

Anne Arundel County Historical Society. *Hand Book of the City of Annapolis and the U. S. Naval Academy.* Annapolis: Maryland Republican Steam Press, 1888.

Banning, Kendall. *Annapolis Today.* Annapolis: U. S. Naval Institute Press, 1957.

Brown, Philip L. *A Century of Separate But Equal Education in Anne Arundel County.* New York: Vantape Press, Inc., 1988.

Duval, Ruby R. *Guide to Historic Annapolis and the U. S. Naval Academy.* Baltimore: Norman, Remington Co., 1926.

Evening Capital (Annapolis). Selected issues, 1884–1939.

Evening Sun (Baltimore). Selected issues, 1910–1972.

Flood, John J. "Echoes of the Past." Annapolis, 1983. Typescript.

Hall, Cary, ed. *The Drags' Handbook.* Annapolis: *The Log* of the United States Naval Academy, [c. 1940].

Home Owners' Loan Corporation. *Valuation Analysis and Conclusions: Extension of the U. S. Naval Academy.* June 25, 1941. Typescript.

House, Arthur E. "From Steam to Electric to Diesel to . . . ?" *Railroading*, 51 (Third Quarter 1974): 16–23.

Jackson, Elmer M., Jr. *Annapolis.* Annapolis: Capital-Gazette Press, 1936.

Jensen, Ann. "The Greeks in Annapolis." *Annapolitan*, October 1988.

———. "The Jews in Annapolis: Transitions and Traditions." *Annapolitan*, July 1989.

———. "Remembering Hell Point." *Annapolitan*, November 1989.

Kieffer, Roxanna White. Personal papers.

Maryland Republican (Annapolis), October 21, 1883.

Mayor's Report. Annapolis, February 11, 1901.

Mayor's Report. Annapolis, June 30, 1902.

McIntire, Robert Harry. *Annapolis, Maryland, Families.* Baltimore: Gateway Press, Inc., 1980.

McWilliams, Jane Wilson, and Carol Cushard Patterson. *Bay Ridge on the Chesapeake.* Annapolis: Brighton Editions, 1986.

Nolley, Ralph F. *The Boys of Annapolis and Anne Arundel Co. Who are Serving Uncle Sam.* Baltimore: Maryland War Record Portrait Books, 1918.

Official Program of the Maryland State Firemen's Association 35th Annual Convention. Annapolis, 1927.

Paynter, William K. *St. Anne's, Annapolis: History and Times.* Annapolis: St. Anne's Parish, 1980.

Polk's Annapolis Directory. New York: R.L. Polk and Co., 1924.

Polk's Annapolis Directory. New York: R.L. Polk and Co., 1928.

Polk's Annapolis Directory. New York: R.L. Polk and Co., 1939.

Programme: Annapolis Fire Department's Super-Fete and Tournament, July 18–25, 1925. Annapolis: Art Press, 1925.

Rambler Athletic Club Football Program. Annapolis, 1937.

Report of Governor Harry W. Nice to the Maryland General Assembly [Special Session, 1936] in Connection with the Rebuilding, Remodeling and Refurnishing of the Executive Mansion. Baltimore: 20th Century Printing Co., 1936.

Report of Thomas Martin, Mayor of the City of Annapolis. Annapolis: J. Guest King, 1881.

Ridgely, David. *Annals of Annapolis.* Baltimore: Cushing and Brother, 1841.

Riley, Elihu S. *History of Anne Arundel County.* Annapolis: Charles G. Feldmeyer, 1905.

Smith, J. Winfree. *A Search for the Liberal College.* Annapolis: St. John's College Press, 1983.

Soley, James Russell. *Historical Sketch of the United States Naval Academy.* Washington: Government Printing Office, 1876.

Souvenir Program of Independent Fire Company No. 2. Annapolis, July 4, 1904.

Sun (Baltimore). Selected issues, 1905–1970.

Sweetman, Jack. *The U. S. Naval Academy: An Illustrated History.* Annapolis: U. S. Naval Institute Press, 1979.

Taylor, Owen M. *The History of Annapolis.* Baltimore: Turnbull Brothers, 1872.

Telephone Directory, Annapolis District, February 1, 1909. Chesapeake and Potomac Telephone Company, 1909.

Telephone Directory for Annapolis 1947-1948. Baltimore: Chesapeake and Potomac Telephone Company of Baltimore City, 1947.

Tilghman, Oswald. *History of Ye Ancient City and Its Public Buildings.* Annapolis: Capital-Gazette Press, n.d.

Tilghman, Tench Francis. *The Early History of St. John's College in Annapolis.* Annapolis: St. John's College Press, 1984.

200 Years with the Maryland Gazette. Annapolis: Capital-Gazette Newspapers, 1927.

U. S. Department of Commerce, Bureau of the Census. *1930 Census of Distribution: Annapolis, Maryland.* Washington: Government Printing Office, 1931.

Warren, Mame, and Marion E. Warren. *Maryland Time Exposures, 1840–1940.* Baltimore: Johns Hopkins University Press, 1984.

Warren, Marion E., and Mame Warren. *The Train's Done Been and Gone: An Annapolis Portrait, 1859–1910.* Boston: David R. Godine, 1976.

Narrators

The numerals that appear at the end of each oral history selection refer to the following interviews conducted by Sharie Valerio, Beth Whaley and Mame Warren:

1. Lillian Fisher, August 1989.
2. Israel "Sonny" Greengold, April 9, 1990.
3. Robert H. Campbell, April 4, 1990.
4. John J. Flood, January 19, 1990.
5. Ibid.
6. Jane Wilson McWilliams, February 17, 1990.
7. Sadie Levy Snyder, March 31, 1990.
8. Thomas C. Worthington, Jr., December 19, 1989.
9. Charles R. Dodds, April 15, 1990.
10. Henry M. Robert III, April 19, 1990.
11. Margaret M. Worthington, February 16, 1990.
12. James Lacey Evans, March 1, 1990.
13. Lester R. Trott, January 22, 1990.
14. Thomas C. Worthington, Jr., December 19, 1989.
15. Carroll H. Hynson, Jr., January 22, 1990.
16. Marion Sherman Borsodi, January 24, 1990.
17. Bernard F. "Bunny" Gessner, April 6, 1990.
18. Henry Holland, February 22, 1990.
19. Sadie Levy Snyder, March 31, 1990.
20. John J. Flood, January 19, 1990.
21. Lester R. Trott, January 22, 1990.
22. Ethelda "Peggy" Brooks Kimbo, April 28, 1990.
23. Bernard F. "Bunny" Gessner, April 6, 1990.
24. Margaret F. Green, January 15, 1990.
25. Marion Sherman Borsodi, January 24, 1990.
26. Mary Lee O'Neill Schab, February 22, 1990.
27. Thomas C. Worthington, Jr., December 19, 1989.
28. Mary Lee O'Neill Schab, February 22, 1990.
29. Margaret Moss Dowsett, February 9, 1990.
30. Robert H. Campbell, April 4, 1990.
31. Bernard F. "Bunny" Gessner, April 6, 1990.

32. Wendell Dean Sears, March 26, 1990.
33. Margaret "Pat" Strange Hayward, February 9, 1990.
34. John J. Flood, January 19, 1990.
35. Dorothy Purvis Thomas, February 9, 1990.
36. Bernard F. "Bunny" Gessner, April 6, 1990.
37. Flora Peterson Chambers, November 20, 1989.
38. Jack Ladd Carr, February 3, 1990.
39. Charles Haste, April 13, 1990.
40. Flora Peterson Chambers, November 20, 1989.
41. Claudia Graham Cullimore, March 22, 1990.
42. Lillian Fisher, August 1989.
43. Thomas C. Worthington, Jr., January 19, 1990.
44. Claudia Graham Cullimore, March 22, 1990.
45. Lester R. Trott, January 22, 1990.
46. Margaret "Missy" Weems Dodds, March 9, 1990.
47. William G. Phelps, April 2, 1990.
48. James B. Collins, February 8, 1990.
49. James Lacey Evans, March 1, 1990.
50. Bernard F. "Bunny" Gessner, April 6, 1990.
51. James Lacey Evans, March 1, 1990.
52. Sadie Levy Snyder, March 31, 1990.
53. Charles Haste, April 13, 1990.
54. Bernard F. "Bunny" Gessner, April 6, 1990.
55. Margaret Moss Dowsett, February 9, 1990.
56. Bernard F. "Bunny" Gessner, April 6, 1990.
57. Ibid.
58. Ibid.
59. Ibid.
60. Henry M. Robert III, April 19, 1990.
61. Jack Ladd Carr, February 3, 1990.
62. Lester R. Trott, January 22, 1990.
63. John J. Flood, January 19, 1990.

64. Thomas C. Worthington, Jr., December 19, 1989.
65. Marjorie Wells, February 9, 1990.
66. Lester R. Trott, January 22, 1990.
67. Margaret F. Green, January 15, 1990.
68. Jack Ladd Carr, February 3, 1990.
69. James Wesley Clark, March 20, 1990.
70. Henry M. Robert III, April 19, 1990.
71. Alexander J. Eucare, April 28, 1990.
72. Israel "Sonny" Greengold, April 9, 1990.
73. Wendell Dean Sears, March 26, 1990.
74. Helen Virginia Rayhart Chambers, April 17, 1990.
75. Henry Holland, February 22, 1990.
76. Carroll H. Hynson, Jr., January 22, 1990.
77. Thomas C. Worthington, Jr., December 19, 1989.
78. Charles R. Dodds, April 15, 1990.
79. Anna Eisenstein Greenberg, April 17, 1990.
80. Henry M. Robert III, April 19, 1990.
81. Anna Eisenstein Greenberg, April 17, 1990.
82. James Lacey Evans, March 1, 1990.
83. Gina Rogers, July 5, 1989.
84. John J. Flood, January 19, 1990.
85. Roger P. "Pip" Moyer, May 10, 1990.
86. Cleo J. Apostol, April 20, 1990.
87. Sadie Levy Snyder, March 31, 1990.
88. Sharie Laccy Valerio, March 9, 1990.
89. Marjorie Wells, February 9, 1990.
90. William J. McWilliams, March 23, 1990.
91. Ethelda "Peggy" Brooks Kimbo, April 28, 1990.
92. Jack Ladd Carr, February 3, 1990.
93. Mary Lee O'Neill Schab, February 22, 1990.
94. Thomas C. Worthington, Jr., January 19, 1990.
95. Ibid., December 19, 1989.
96. Lester R. Trott, January 22, 1990.
97. Jane Wilson McWilliams, February 17, 1990.
98. Flora Peterson Chambers, November 20, 1989.

99. Ethelda "Peggy" Brooks Kimbo, April 28, 1990.
100. Thomas M. Branzell, April 27, 1990.
101. Roger P. "Pip" Moyer, May 10, 1990.
102. Lester R. Trott, January 22, 1990.
103. Mary Lee O'Neill Schab, February 22, 1990.
104. Margaret Moss Dowsett, February 9, 1990.
105. Henry M. Robert III, April 19, 1990.
106. Thomas C. Worthington, Jr., January 19, 1990.
107. Margaret Moss Dowsett, February 9, 1990.
108. Alexander J. Eucare, April 28, 1990.
109. Ibid.
110. Wendell Dean Sears, March 26, 1990.
111. Jane Wilson McWilliams, February 17, 1990.
112. Carroll H. Hynson, Jr., January 22, 1990.
113. Mary V. Wiseman, April 30, 1990.
114. Marita Carroll, May 16, 1990.
115. Wendell Dean Sears, March 26, 1990.
116. Ethelda "Peggy" Brooks Kimbo, April 28, 1990.
117. James Wesley Clark, March 20, 1990.
118. Margaret F. Green, January 15, 1990.
119. Carroll H. Hynson, Jr., January 22, 1990.
120. Thomas M. Branzell, April 27, 1990.
121. Carroll H. Hynson, Jr., January 22, 1990.
122. Margaret F. Green, January 15, 1990.
123. Gina Rogers, July 5, 1989.
124. Flora Peterson Chambers, November 20, 1989.
125. Ibid.
126. Henry M. Robert III, April 19, 1990.
127. Jane Wilson McWilliams, February 17, 1990.
128. Ethelda "Peggy" Brooks Kimbo, April 28, 1990.
129. Thomas C. Worthington, Jr., January 19, 1990.
130. James Wesley Clark, March 20, 1990.
131. Sharie Lacey Valerio, March 9, 1990.
132. Jane Wilson McWilliams, June 30, 1990.
133. Sharie Lacey Valerio, March 9, 1990.
134. Thomas C. Worthington, Jr., December 19, 1989.
135. Sharie Lacey Valerio, March 9, 1990.
136. Jane Wilson McWilliams, February 17, 1990.
137. Jack Ladd Carr, February 3, 1990.
138. Sadie Levy Snyder, March 31, 1990.
139. Jack Ladd Carr, February 3, 1990.
140. Sharie Lacey Valerio, March 9, 1990.
141. Alexander J. Eucare, April 28, 1990.
142. Flora Peterson Chambers, November 20, 1989.
143. Marjorie Wells, February 9, 1990.
144. Marion E. Warren, June 27, 1990.
145. Robert H. Campbell, April 4, 1990.
146. Ibid.
147. Lester R. Trott, January 22, 1990.
148. Roger P. "Pip" Moyer, May 10, 1990.
149. Ibid.
150. Jack Ladd Carr, February 3, 1990.
151. Mame Warren, March 8, 1990.
152. Mary V. Wiseman, April 30, 1990.
153. Charles Haste, April 13, 1990.
154. Roger P. "Pip" Moyer, May 10, 1990.
155. Ethelda "Peggy" Brooks Kimbo, April 28, 1990.
156. Carroll H. Hynson, Jr., January 22, 1990.
157. Mame Warren, March 8, 1990.
158. Jane Wilson McWilliams, February 17, 1990.
159. Israel "Sonny" Greengold, April 9, 1990.
160. George Phelps, July 17, 1990.
161. Wendell Dean Sears, March 26, 1990.
162. A. St. Clair Wright, April 23, 1990.
163. Claudia Graham Cullimore, March 22, 1990.
164. Carroll H. Hynson, Jr., January 22, 1990.
165. Israel "Sonny" Greengold, April 9, 1990.
166. Mary V. Wiseman, April 30, 1990.
167. Lester R. Trott, January 22, 1990.
168. Margaret Moss Dowsett, February 9, 1990.
169. Henry M. Robert III, February 17, 1990.
170. Jane Wilson McWilliams, February 17, 1990.
171. Roger P. "Pip" Moyer, May 10, 1990.
172. Bernard F. "Bunny" Gessner, April 6, 1990.
173. Ibid.
174. Jack Ladd Carr, February 3, 1990.
175. Claudia Graham Cullimore, March 22, 1990.
176. Jane Wilson McWilliams, February 17, 1990.
177. Bernard F. "Bunny" Gessner, April 6, 1990.
178. Anna Eisenstein Greenberg, April 17, 1990.
179. Margaret F. Green, January 15, 1990.
180. Israel "Sonny" Greengold, April 9, 1990.
181. Marita Carroll, May 16, 1990.
182. Jack Ladd Carr, February 3, 1990.
183. Thomas C. Worthington, Jr., December 19, 1989.

Index

Page references to illustrations appear in italics; references to oral history selections are in bold.

210

Photograph Credits

Photographer Tom Baden posed for his own camera in his darkroom, circa 1953. The work area was located in the basement of his Capitol Hill Manor home. MdHR G 2140–459

THEN AGAIN...

This book was composed in Palatino by Electronic Publishing Solutions,
Annapolis, Maryland, from a design by Gerard A. Valerio.
It was printed on 80-lb. Lithofect by Whitmore Printing Company,
Annapolis, Maryland, and bound in Holliston Kingston Linen (*casebound*)
by Advantage Book Binding, Inc., Glen Burnie, Maryland.